Boutique Casual

for BOYS & GIRLS

17 Timeless Projects • Full-Size Clothing Patterns
Sizes 12 months to 5 years

Sue Kim

stash BOOKS®

an imprint of C&T Publishing

Text and Artwork copyright © 2014 by Sue Kim

Photography and Artwork copyright © 2014 by C&T Publishing, Inc.

Publisher: Amy Marson

Creative Director: Gailen Runge

Art Director/Book Designer:
Kristy Zacharias

Editor: Liz Aneloski

Technical Editors: Alison M. Schmidt and
Mary E. Flynn

Page Layout Artist: Kristen Yenche

Production Coordinator: Jenny Davis

Production Editor: Joanna Burgarino

Illustrator: Jessica Jenkins

Photo Assistant: Mary Peyton Peppo

Styled photos by Nissa Brehmer, unless
otherwise noted; Instructional photos
by Diane Pedersen, unless otherwise
noted; How-to photos by Sue Kim,
unless otherwise noted

Published by Stash Books, an imprint of C&T Publishing, Inc., P.O. Box 1456,
Lafayette, CA 94549

Contents

Dedication

To those hearts that are diligently sewing the perfect handmade outfit for that special person. If it were not for those sewists and their will to create, this book would not exist. I dedicate this book to those sewists and to future readers who will experience the unique joy of making handmade clothing!

Acknowledgments

Although I am a sewing mom, I don't always have the chance to make clothes for my daughter. However, when I do find the time to make a dress, a skirt, or even a simple tee, it's always worth it. She is sure to express her thanks and excitement whenever possible: to her friends, to the family, and of course—to me!

I would like to thank my husband, Jung, who always puts me at the top of his priorities, and my three children, Chan, Caleb, and Veronica—my stars forever! And a special thanks to Veronica for helping me tremendously while I was working on the designs for the book.

Another thanks to June and Calvin, my dear friends who are always quietly and cheerfully helping me, whatever the need. And to John, who helped me with processing the patterns, as well as Christine, who makes me smile. I also want to mention my friends Patrick, Betty, and Glenda for their support and assistance.

In addition, I want to thank my dear friend Thelma and her daughter, Isabelle, who was kind enough to try on the patterns for this book! I missed you both throughout the whole process of writing this book, and I wish little Isabelle a happy, healthy future. Special thanks to my sewing buddies Hye Kyung, Jung and Young Mi, Yoon, who helped make the samples and provided wise advice.

A special thanks to Cloud9 Fabrics, Fat Quarter Shop, Riley Blake Designs, and Michael Miller Fabrics for providing fabrics of excellent quality for the garments in this book!

Finally, a big thank-you to Liz, Alison, and the publishers for guiding me through the whole process and for making the book-writing experience so pleasant.

Introduction

Only a century ago, all the clothes we wore were sewn by our mothers, grandmothers, and aunts. Sewing has skipped a generation, or more, in many families, so most of us did not grow up watching clothing being made. Maybe this is why so many sewists are intimidated by the thought of sewing clothing.

Many people have asked me the question, "Isn't it difficult to sew clothing?" My reply is the same every time: "Women throughout history have done it, so why can't we?" We feel challenged, not because it is impossible, but because we have never done it before.

Many thought elastic-waist pants were difficult to make, but when I showed how to make them using my simple, beginner-friendly pattern, the same people always agreed: "Wow! That was easy!"

One of my goals in writing this book is to make sewing clothes less intimidating and more approachable. I want to help the reader overcome fear and open up a brand new world in which sewists of all levels can make their own perfect apparel. Just try some of these patterns; you'll see how easy they are.

Boutique Casual for Boys & Girls

The Basics

Choosing Fabrics

When making clothing, it is important to choose the fabric type based on the garment and its intended use, so please refer to the chart below when considering your options.

I used mostly easy-to-obtain, lightweight cotton and quilting-weight cotton for the samples in this book. Cotton is very comfortable and is efficient at absorbing sweat, so it is a great option for children's clothing. Linen/cotton blend fabric works very well for dresses, pants, and coats. Denim is a common material for pants, but it also works great for dresses and

jackets; besides purchasing brand-new fabric, consider recycling old jeans! Single knit/jersey fabrics are most often used for making T-shirts, while heavier double knit is preferred for jogging suits. Lightweight corduroy is another versatile option when you need warmth. Also, consider using laminated cotton to make waterproof jackets.

It is wise to prewash all fabrics used in garment making. It prevents shrinkage and dye bleeding in the finished garment. Iron using the manufacturer's instructions, which are usually printed on the end of the bolt of fabric.

	DRESSES/SKIRTS	BLOUSES	PANTS/SHORTS	T-SHIRTS	COATS/JACKETS
Lightweight Cotton	*	*			
Quilting-Weight Cotton	*	*	*		*
Linen/Cotton Blend	*		*		*
Denim	*		*		*
Single Knit/Jersey	*	*		*	
Double Knit			*		*
Corduroy	*		*		*
Laminated Cotton					*

Pattern Symbols

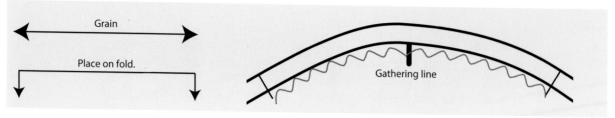

Grain

Place on fold.

Gathering line

Pattern Notches

Notch the triangular point marked on the pattern to make matching the pattern pieces easy. Be careful not to notch too deep into the seam allowance! You can also cut the notch outward to avoid that.

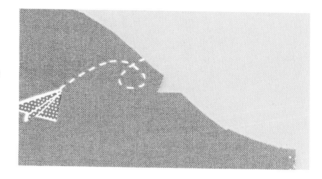

NOTE

Please use the measurements in the chart below when choosing what size garment to make. The sizes of sewing patterns can vary from those of ready-to-wear clothing found in stores.

SIZE CHART

	12 Months	18 Months	24 Months	3 Years	4 Years	5 Years
Height	31½˝	33¾˝	36˝	38¾˝	41½˝	43½˝
Chest	21˝	21½˝	22˝	22½˝	23˝	23½˝
Waist	19¾˝	20⅛˝	20½˝	21˝	21½˝	22˝
Hip	21˝	21⅞˝	22¾˝	23¾˝	24˝	25˝

Tracing the Patterns

The patterns in this book are printed with multiple sizes together on the pattern pullouts. You will need to trace the pieces for the size garment you are making onto your own paper. Place tracing paper on top of the pattern and position sewing weights to hold the paper in place. Trace the pattern lines onto the tracing paper and write down all important numbers and instructions.

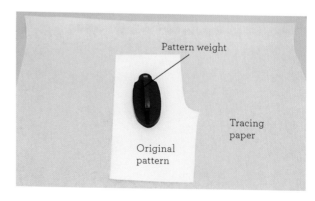

Pattern weight

Tracing paper

Original pattern

Some pattern pieces have style variations in the neck, collar, or closure. Some can be cut in multiple lengths. Follow the cutting instructions for each project and the notes on the pattern pieces to trace and cut the directed shape or length. You can also use this feature to make any short-sleeve top into a long-sleeve top.

 It can be difficult to tell the difference between the right and wrong sides of solid-colored fabrics. Once you figure out which is which, mark the right side using a washable pen.

Cutting Layouts

Fold the fabric as shown in the cutting layout and then place the pattern on the folded fabric or a single layer, as indicated. Cut out the pieces. These cutting layouts assume a directional print. Depending on the size you are making, or if your fabric is not a directional print, you may be able to place your pattern pieces closer together, which will require less fabric.

However, for stripes, plaids, or large graphic prints, I encourage you to purchase extra fabric and carefully arrange the pattern pieces on the fabric so that the fabric design will match when the garment is sewn together.

Finishing Seams

The seam allowances of clothing need to be finished to ensure that during use or laundering they do not ravel or fray, or else the seams could come apart.

One method to finish the seams is to use a serger. However, if you do not own a serger, use the zigzag stitch on a regular sewing machine.

Finish the seam allowances after you stitch each seam. You do not need to finish the hems or necklines.

Choosing Needles and Threads

Choose needle and thread sizes based on the fabric you intend to use. Generally, for threads, the higher the number, the thinner the thread. However, for needles, the higher the number, the thicker the needle.

In most cases, size 11 or 12 needles are best suited for lighter-weight fabrics such as quilting-weight cotton, while thicker fabrics like denim and corduroy stitch better with a size 14 needle. When sewing jersey or single knit fabric, use a jersey or ball point needle.

TIP If you're a confident sewist, are certain of the fit, and don't need the notches for matching, finish the edges that will be seamed together before sewing any two pieces together.

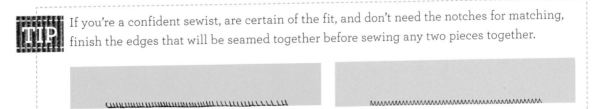

Serged edge

Zigzagged edge

Making Bias Strips

Using a ruler and cutting mat, cut strips at a 45° angle to the straight of the grain or selvage (*Figures A and B*). Place two strips at a 90° angle to each other and with right sides together. Mark a stitching line ¼″ from the diagonal edges, pin, and sew on the line (*Figure C*). Check to be sure your sewing line is at the correct angle by opening the strips to make sure you are making a long, straight strip. Add more strips until you have the desired length, and then trim off the leftover corners and press all the seams open.

For neckline trim, use the strips as you cut them. For sleeve hems, follow these instructions to fold and press the strips.

Fold the strip in half lengthwise, wrong sides together. Open the strip, fold the long edges toward the center, crease, and press (*Figure D*). Fold in half again and press.

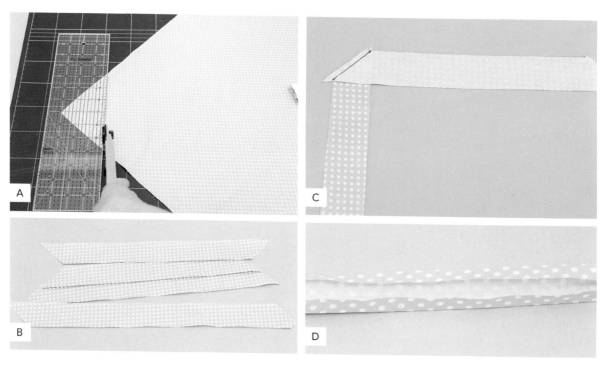

A

B

C

D

Using a Bias Maker

If you are making a lot of folded bias strips, it helps to have a bias tape maker. Follow the manufacturer's instructions to cut strips the correct width for the finished size you desire.

1. Using a sharp tool, push the bias strip into the bias tape maker. *Figure A*

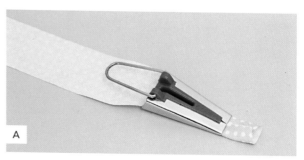

A

2. Pull the bias tape through the bias tape maker and press. *Figure B*

3. Fold it in half again and press to make double-fold bias tape. *Figure C*

Trimming with Bias Strips

1. Align the folded bias strip, right side down, with the edge of the garment piece to be trimmed, wrong side up. Pin and stitch the bias strip, along the bottom fold line, to the garment piece. *Figure A*

2. Wrap the bias strip over to the right side of the piece, folding the raw edge of the bias down inside the bias strip. Pin and sew the bias strip ⅛˝ from the upper edge as shown—this is called *edgestitching*. *Figures B & C*

 TIP If you are a confident sewist, encase the raw edge you wish to trim with the double-fold bias strip, and edgestitch through all layers at once.

Sleeve, wrong side up

Folded bias strip, wrong side up

Stitch on fold.

A

Bias strip sewn to wrong side of sleeve

C

Edgestitch

Finished hem

B

Fold bias over to right side of sleeve.

Bias strip folded over to right side of sleeve

Making Buttonholes

Buttonhole placement is determined by the gender of the person wearing the garment. When making apparel for girls, make the buttonholes on the right-hand side of the clothing; use the left-hand side for boys.

Girls' buttonhole   Boys' buttonhole

Refer to your sewing machine manual or the machine manufacturer's website for instructions on making buttonholes.

 TIP Once the stitching has been completed, place a pin through the stitching across the top of the buttonhole. Inside the bottom stitches, poke your seam ripper into the opposite end and push toward the pin that you inserted at the top. It will neatly cut the buttonhole and stop at the pin, without overcutting.

 TIP Although many sewists love to add buttons to their clothing projects, buttonhole stitching is a time-consuming and sometimes difficult process. If you would like to simplify this whole process and don't mind the investment in a few simple tools, you can use snaps instead. Follow the instructions that come with the snap setter tool.

Using Elastic

Pants and dresses usually use woven elastic bands. Since these bands are very stretchy and smooth, they are quite the suitable choice.

The elasticity varies from elastic to elastic, so I can only give recommended lengths. Add or subtract length from this number depending on the elastic you are using. The recommended elastic length is about 80%–90% of the waist size.

Recommended Waist Elastic Length

	12 Months	18 Months	24 Months	3 Years	4 Years	5 Years
Elastic Length	19″	19¼″	19½″	19¾″	20″	20¼″

Recommended Thigh Elastic Length

	12 Months	18 Months	24 Months	3 Years	4 Years	5 Years
Elastic Length	11¾″	11¾″	12″	12¼″	12¾″	13¼″

Making the Casing for Elastic Bands

1. Fold the waist over ⅜˝ to the wrong side and press. *Figure A*

2. Fold the waist over an additional 1⅝˝ to the wrong side and press. *Figure B*

3. Edgestitch around the upper and lower folds to make the casing, leaving a 2˝ opening to insert the elastic at the back.

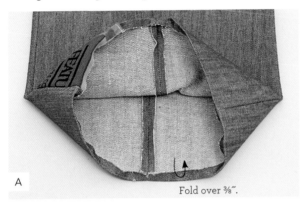

A

Fold over ⅜˝.

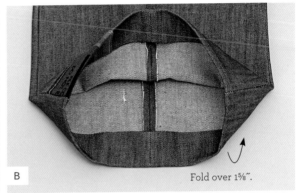

B

Fold over 1⅝˝.

Inserting Elastic into a Casing

1. Attach a safety pin to an end of the elastic. *Figure A*

2. Insert the safety pin into an open end of the casing. *Figure B*

3. Push and pull the safety pin until it comes out of the other end of the casing.

4. Overlap the ends, sew the elastic together in a box shape, and cut off the excess elastic. *Figure C*

5. Use a pointed tool (like scissors or a letter opener) to push the end of the elastic back into the casing. Stitch the opening closed. *Figure D*

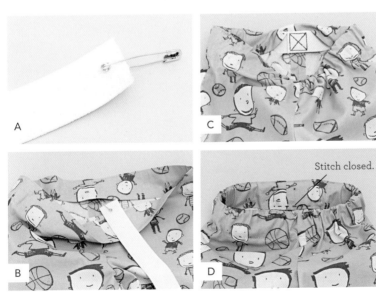

A

C

B

D

Stitch closed.

Making Gathers

1. Lengthen your machine's stitch to a basting stitch (usually the longest stitch on your sewing machine). Stitch 2 lines of basting stitches from the first end of the gathering line to the other end, leaving a length of thread at either end.

2. Pull the threads from 1 end to make the gathers and adjust the length of the piece.

3. Place a pin at 1 end, and wind the thread on the pin in a figure eight. Adjust the gathers to make this piece the same length as the piece you are attaching it to. Pin the other side, winding the thread on the pin. *Figures A & B*

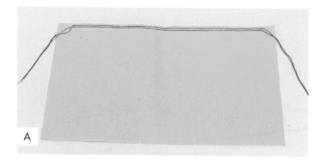

A

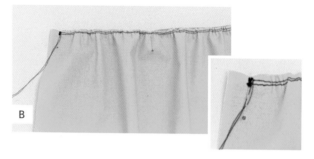

B

Attaching a Gathered Skirt to a Bodice

1. Refer to Making Gathers (above) to gather the top edge of the skirt. Before pulling the gathering threads, mark the top edge in quarters (center front, center back, and both side seams) with pins.

2. Mark the bodice in quarters in the same manner. Place the bodice inside the skirt, right sides together, and match and pin the 4 points. *Figure A*

3. Adjust the gathers between the 4 points so the skirt fits the bodice. Pin and stitch all around with a ⅜″ seam allowance. *Figure B*

A

B

Sewing a Hem

1. Patterns include a 1½″ hem allowance. You can also adjust the hem as desired. Fold the hem up by half the desired hem amount, with wrong sides together, and press. *Figure A*

2. Fold up the same amount again and press. Stitch the hem close to the upper folded edge. *Figure B*

A

Fold once.

B

Stitch. Fold again.

Hemming Option

After cutting out the fabric pieces, press the hems on the sleeves, pant legs, and front and back pieces to make assembly much easier.

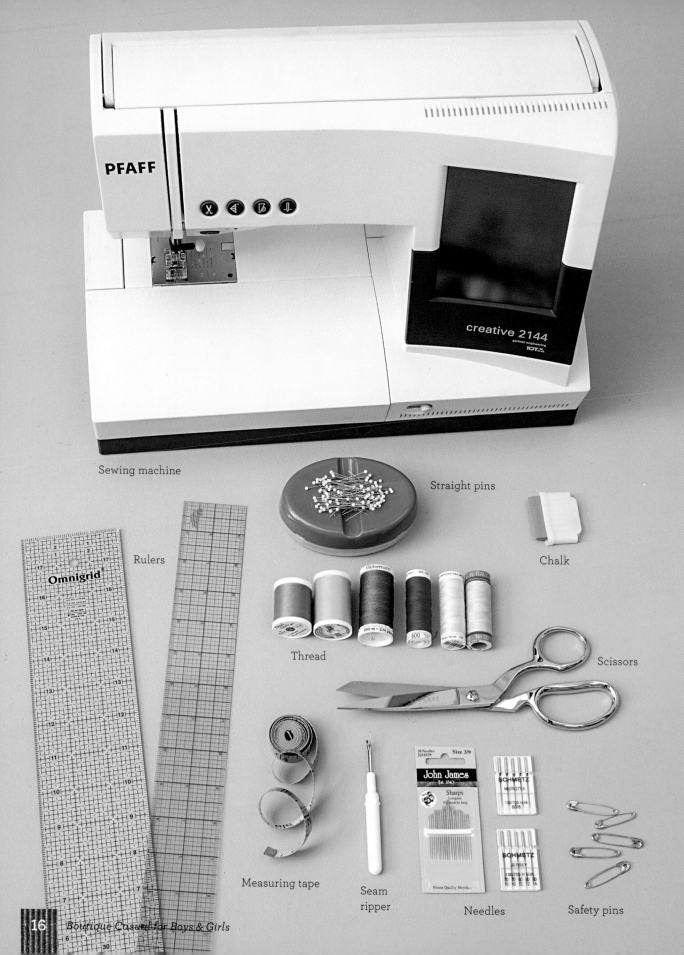

Sewing machine

Straight pins

Chalk

Rulers

Thread

Scissors

Measuring tape

Seam ripper

Needles

Safety pins

Decorating a Garment

To make solid-colored T-shirts more interesting, try drawing or printing your own artwork onto transfer paper. Transfer paper is simple to use because all you need to do is iron it onto the T-shirt. Lesley Riley's TAP Transfer Artist Paper (C&T Publishing) is a great product for this process. Even beginners can make beautifully customized T-shirts without any difficulty. *Figure A*

A

Another way to add style to T-shirts is by using hot-fix foils, rhinestones, or studs. These sticker-like beads are also easy to apply—they need only to be ironed on! *Figure B*

Other decorative items include patches and labels. There are two different kinds of patches; one is ironed on and the other is sewn on. Letter and number patches are especially fun to use. *Figures C & D*

B

There are cotton and leather labels. Leather labels complement denim or cargo pants. The majority of the leather labels currently being sold do not require a special needle to sew them onto the clothing. *Figure E*

C

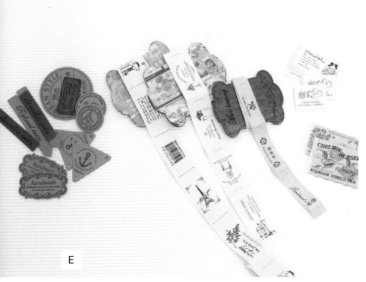

E

D

Charlotte Dress

SKILL LEVEL: Intermediate *** | SIZE: 12 months–5 years

With puffed sleeves, a rounded collar, and tiny gathers, the Charlotte Dress is the very essence of cuteness. It can be worn all year round and can be casual or semiformal. As a result, it can be worn on numerous occasions, ranging from outdoor play dates to dinner parties. The rounded collar gives it a traditional look, making it a perfect match with Mary Jane shoes.

MATERIALS

- 1⅔ yards 44˝-wide fabric or 1½ yards 58˝-wide fabric for dress

- ⅓ yard 44˝-wide or 58˝-wide fabric for lining

- ¼ yard or 1 fat quarter for contrast collar (*optional*)

- ¼ yard lightweight fusible interfacing, 20˝ wide, for collar (*optional*)

- 3 buttons (½˝ / 12mm) or snaps

CUTTING

Trace each pattern piece in the desired size and transfer any markings (see Tracing the Patterns, page 8). Cut out the pieces, referring to the appropriate cutting layout for placement. Optional: Finish the front, back, sleeve, and skirt seams in advance (see Finishing Seams, page 9).

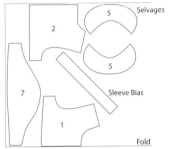

44˝-wide fabric suggested cutting layout

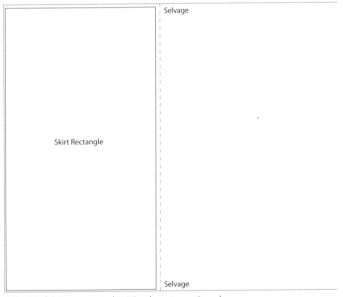

44˝-wide fabric suggested cutting layout, continued

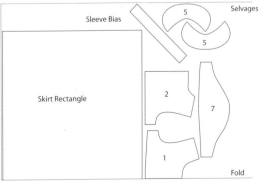

58˝-wide fabric suggested cutting layout

Dress fabric

- Cut 1 Front 1 on fold (use the line labeled "medium" as the bottom cutting line).

- Cut 2 Back 2 (medium).

- Cut 2 Sleeve 7 (short).

- Cut 1 rectangle for the skirt in the size you've chosen*:

  12 mos: 16˝ × 42˝

  18 mos: 17⅝˝ × 44˝

  24 mos: 19⅛˝ × 46˝

  3 yrs: 20⅝˝ × 48˝

  4 yrs: 22⅛˝ × 50˝

  5 yrs: 23⅝˝ × 52˝

For larger sizes, if you are using a 44˝-wide directional print, you may need to adjust the cutting layout so that the prints match or use additional yardage to piece the skirt.

- Cut 2 bias strips for sleeve trim 1¾˝ wide by the length listed for the size you've chosen:

  12 mos: 9½˝

  18 mos: 9¾˝

  24 mos: 10˝

  3 yrs: 10¼˝

  4 yrs: 10½˝

  5 yrs: 10¾˝

Lining fabric

- Cut 1 Front 1 on fold (medium).

- Cut 2 Back 2 (medium).

Collar fabric

- Cut 4 Collar 5.

Interfacing

- Cut 2 Collar 5 (*optional*).

- Read through all the project instructions before beginning to sew.

- A ⅜˝ seam allowance is included on the pattern—sew with a ⅜˝ seam allowance unless otherwise noted. A 1½˝ hem is included in the dress.

- Backstitch at the beginning and end of each seam.

- Press after sewing each seam. Finish seams as desired.

Making the Collar

1. If you add interfacing, follow the manufacturer's instructions to fuse the interfacing on the wrong side of 1 collar piece for each pair.

2. Place 2 collar pieces right sides together, and pin and sew along the outer edge.

3. Notch the curved seam allowances (by cutting away small triangles of fabric within the seam allowance). This reduces bulk so the curve will lie flat. Be careful not to cut the stitching. *Figure A*

4. Turn right side out and press. *Figure B*

5. Repeat Steps 1–4 with the remaining 2 collar pieces.

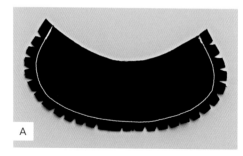

A

B

Assembling the Bodice and Lining

1. Place the bodice front and both bodice back pieces right sides together, aligning the raw edges at the shoulders. Pin and sew along the shoulder seams.

2. Press the seams open.

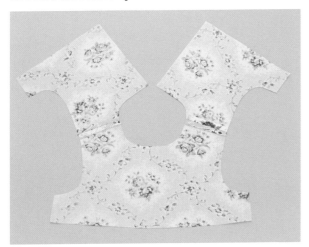

3. Repeat Steps 1 and 2 with the bodice lining pieces.

FRONT

BACK

CHARLOTTE DRESS INSPIRATION

4. Place the collars on the right side of the bodice neckline, overlapping them at the center front so that they meet perfectly at the ⅜″ seamline. Pin, easing as needed, and baste the collars in place. *Figure A*

5. Place the bodice lining on the bodice with right sides together. Align and pin along the center back and neckline. Stitch as shown. *Figure B*

6. Clip the seam allowance (by cutting tiny slits) on the neckline seam, being careful not to clip the stitching. This allows the seam allowance to spread out around the curve. *Figure C*

7. Turn right side out and press. *Figure D*

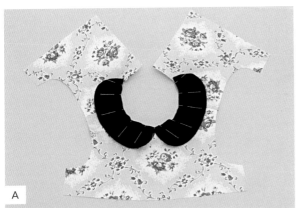

A

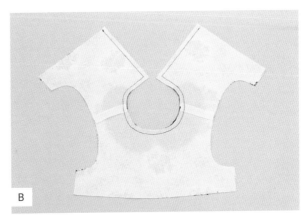

B

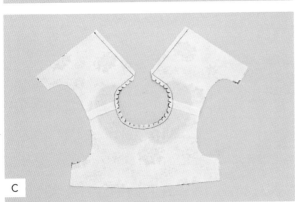

C

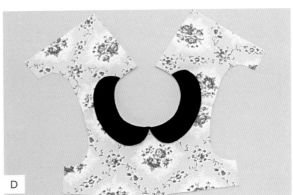

D

Making and Attaching the Sleeves

1. Fold and press the bias strips for the sleeves (see Making Bias Strips, page 10).

2. Gather the sleeve along the gathering lines at the top and along the entire length of the bottom edge (see Making Gathers, page 14). *Figure A*

3. Adjust the gathers on the bottom edge of the sleeve to match the length of the bias strip.

4. Hem the sleeve with the bias strip (see Trimming with Bias Strips, page 11)

5. Repeat Steps 2–4 for the other sleeve.

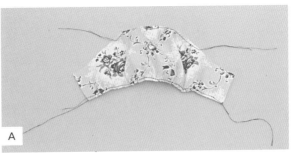

A

6. Pin the curved top edge of the sleeve to the bodice front and back, right sides together, starting with the center and ends.

7. Adjust the gathers evenly.

8. Pin the rest of the seam. Sew the sleeve to the bodice. *Figure A*

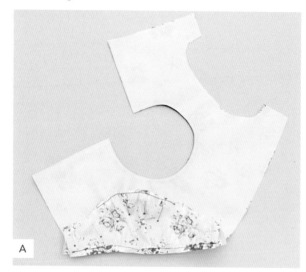

A

9. Repeat Steps 6–8 to attach the other sleeve.

Connecting the Sleeves and Sides

1. Fold the bodice pieces, right sides together, aligning the front and back pieces. Pin and sew the sleeve and side seams, starting at the sleeve. *Figure B*

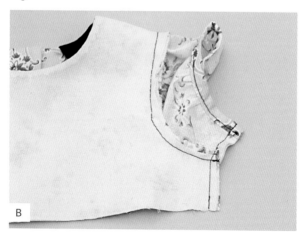

B

2. Turn the bodice right side out, with the back facing up. Overlap the left-hand piece over the right, so that both back and front lie flat. Pin and baste the overlapped back pieces together at the bottom. *Figure C*

C

Making and Attaching the Skirt

1. Fold the skirt piece in half widthwise with right sides together. Pin and sew the center back seam. Press the seam open.

2. Make gathers along the top edge of the skirt (see Making Gathers, page 14). *Figure D*

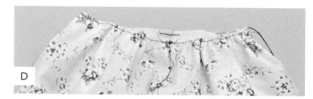

D

3. Pin and sew the skirt to the bodice (see Attaching a Gathered Skirt to a Bodice, page 14), adjusting the gathers to fit the bodice. Sew over the overlapped bodice backs as well.

4. Turn the dress right side out and press lightly.

Finishing the Dress

1. Sew the hem (see Sewing a Hem, page 15).

2. Make 3 buttonholes on the bodice back, centering the buttonholes on the overlap (see Making Buttonholes, page 12). Place the top and bottom buttonholes ½˝ from the edges of the bodice, and space the remaining buttonhole evenly between them. Sew on the buttons. Or, attach the snaps.

Maria Dress

SKILL LEVEL: Confident Beginner ★★ | **SIZE:** 12 months–5 years

The cute puffed sleeves and three-tiered skirt of the Maria Dress allow for lots of activity. The lack of a collar makes this pattern a bit easier to assemble than the Charlotte Dress (page 18). The dress looks great with leggings.

MATERIALS

- 1¾ yards 44˝-wide fabric or 1¼ yards 58˝-wide fabric for dress

- ⅓ yard 44˝-wide or 58˝-wide fabric for lining

- 3 buttons (½˝ / 12mm) or snaps

CUTTING

Trace each pattern piece in the desired size and transfer any markings (see Tracing the Patterns, page 8). Cut out the pieces, referring to the appropriate cutting layout. Optional: Finish the front, back, sleeve, and skirt seams in advance (see Finishing Seams, page 9).

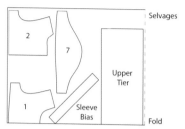

44˝-wide fabric suggested cutting layout, double layer

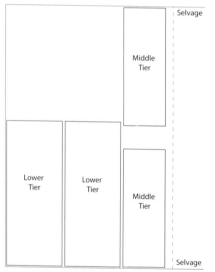

44˝-wide fabric suggested cutting layout, single layer

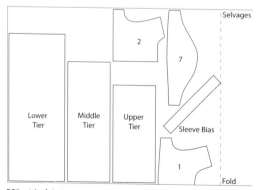

58˝-wide fabric suggested cutting layout

Dress fabric

- Cut 1 Front 1 on fold (medium).
- Cut 2 Back 2 (medium).
- Cut 2 Sleeve 7 (short).
- Cut the rectangles listed for the skirt tiers for the size that you've chosen:

  12 mos: 4¾˝ × 30¼˝ (upper), 2 at 4¾˝ × 18⅞˝ (middle), and 2 at 7¼˝ × 23⅛˝ (lower)

  18 mos: 5¼˝ × 31½˝, 2 at 5¼˝ × 19⅝˝, and 2 at 7¾˝ × 24˝

  24 mos: 5¾˝ × 32¾˝, 2 at 5¾˝ × 20⅜˝, and 2 at 8¼˝ × 24⅜˝

  3 yrs: 6¼˝ × 34˝, 2 at 6¼˝ × 21⅛˝, and 2 at 8¾˝ × 25⅞˝

  4 yrs: 6¾˝ × 35¼˝, 2 at 6¾˝ × 21⅞˝, and 2 at 9¼˝ × 26⅞˝

  5 yrs: 7¼˝ × 36½˝, 2 at 7¼˝ × 22⅝˝, and 2 at 9¾˝ × 27¾˝

- Cut 2 bias strips for sleeve trim 1¾˝ wide by the length listed for the size you've chosen:

  12 mos: 9½˝

  18 mos: 9¾˝

  24 mos: 10˝

  3 yrs: 10¼˝

  4 yrs: 10½˝

  5 yrs: 10¾˝

Lining fabric

- Cut 1 Front 1 on fold (medium).
- Cut 2 Back 2 (medium).

- Read through all the project instructions before beginning to sew.
- A ⅜˝ seam allowance is included on the pattern. A 1½˝ hem is included on the dress.
- Backstitch at the beginning and end of each seam.
- Press after sewing each seam. Finish seams as desired.

Assembling the Bodice and Lining

Follow Steps 1–3 and 6–8 for the Charlotte Dress (Assembling the Bodice and Lining, page 21) to assemble the bodice and lining.

Making and Attaching the Sleeves

Follow steps 1–9 for the Charlotte Dress (Making and Attaching the Sleeves, page 23) to make and attach the sleeves.

Connecting the Sleeves and Sides

Follow Steps 1 and 2 for the Charlotte Dress (Connecting the Sleeves and Sides, page 24) to connect the sleeves and sides.

Making and Attaching the Skirt

1. Fold the upper skirt tier in half widthwise, right sides together. Pin and sew along the short edge to make a loop. Press the seam open.

2. Pin the 2 middle skirt tier rectangles right sides together, along the short ends. Sew both side seams to make a loop. Press the seams open. Repeat this process with the 2 bottom skirt tier rectangles.

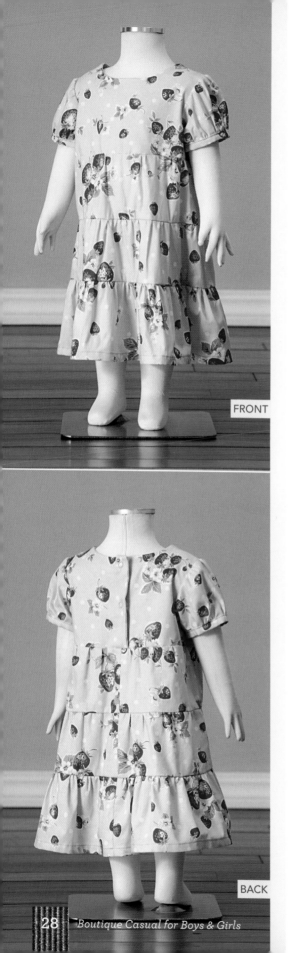

FRONT

BACK

3. Sew gathering stitches along the upper edge of each skirt tier (see Making Gathers, page 14). *Figure A*

A

4. Matching the sides and center front and back first, pin the unstitched edge of the middle tier to the stitched edge of the lower tier, right sides together, as shown. Adjust the gathers to fit and pin all around (see Attaching a Gathered Skirt to a Bodice, page 14). *Figure B*

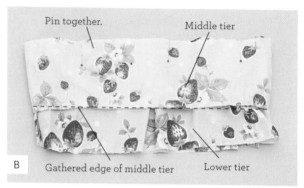

Pin together.   Middle tier

B   Gathered edge of middle tier   Lower tier

5. Sew both tiers together (see Attaching a Gathered Skirt to a Bodice, page 14).

6. Repeat Steps 4 and 5 to attach the upper tier to the middle tier. *Figure C*

7. Sew the hem (see Sewing a Hem, page 15).

C

8. Mark the bodice and the skirt waist in quarters. Pin the bodice and skirt right sides together, adjust the skirt gathers to fit, and sew together. Press the seam allowance upward and topstitch ⅛˝ from the seam (*optional*).

Finishing the Dress

Make 3 buttonholes on the bodice back (see Making Buttonholes, page 12, and Charlotte Dress, Finishing the Dress, page 24, for placement) and sew on the buttons. Or, attach the snaps.

Leanna Blouse

SKILL LEVEL: Confident Beginner ** | SIZE: 12 months–5 years

The Leanna Blouse has puffed sleeves and works well with both pants and skirts, making it the perfect blouse for little girls. Make the blouse from a white fabric and it will match many other items in her wardrobe.

Using lace or embroidered fabric can make the blouse appropriate for formal outings. Or pair this blouse with a black skirt with frills and it could be a delightful combination on the day of her special performance.

MATERIALS

- 1 yard 44″-wide fabric or ⅞ yard 58″-wide fabric for blouse

- 5–7 buttons (½″ / 12mm) or snaps

CUTTING

Trace each pattern piece in the desired size and transfer any markings (see Tracing the Patterns, page 8). On the Back 2 pattern piece, trace the extended center back line as shown.

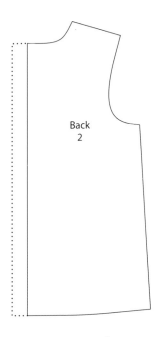

Cut out the pieces, referring to the appropriate cutting layout. Optional: *Finish the front, back, and sleeve seams in advance (see Finishing Seams, page 9).*

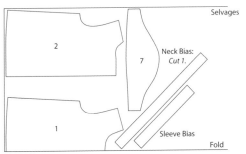

44″-wide fabric suggested cutting layout

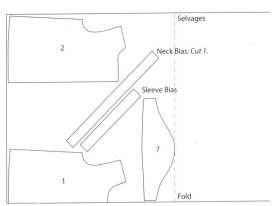

58″-wide fabric suggested cutting layout

Blouse fabric

- Cut 1 Front 1 on fold (long).

- Cut 2 Back 2 (long).

- Cut 2 Sleeve 7 (short).

- Cut 2 bias strips for sleeve trim 1¾˝ wide by the length listed for the size you've chosen:

    12 mos: 9½˝

    18 mos: 9¾˝

    24 mos: 10˝

    3 yrs: 10¼˝

    4 yrs: 10½˝

    5 yrs: 10¾˝

- Cut 1 bias strip for neckline trim 1¾˝ × 19½˝.

- Read through all the project instructions before beginning to sew.

- A ⅜˝ seam allowance is included on the pattern.

- A 1½˝ hem is included on the pattern.

- Backstitch at the beginning and end of each seam.

- Press after sewing each seam. Finish seams as desired.

Assembling the Front and Back

1. Pin the front and back pieces right sides together at the shoulders. Sew the shoulder seams. Press the seams open.

2. Fold over the center back edge of each back piece 1½˝ to the right side and press. *Figure A*

3. Pin the unfolded bias strip all around the neckline, right sides together. Stitch around the neck. Trim any excess bias. *Figure B*

4. Clip the curved seam well. You can also use pinking shears here. *Figure C*

5. Fold the neckline bias over to the wrong side of the blouse. *Figure D*

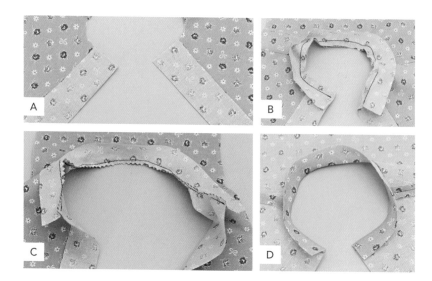

6. Press the bias toward the blouse's wrong side, and then fold and press the loose edge of the bias under. *Figure E*

7. Open the folded center back edges so that the fabric is right side out. Press both edges flat. *Figure F*

8. Pin and stitch the bias trim down all around the neckline, as close to the folded edge as possible. *Figure G*

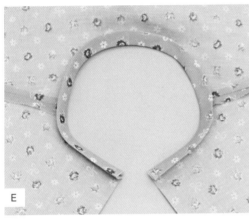

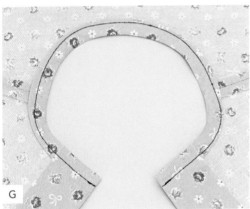

Making and Attaching the Sleeves

Follow Steps 1–9 for the Charlotte Dress (Making and Attaching the Sleeves, page 23) to make and attach the sleeves.

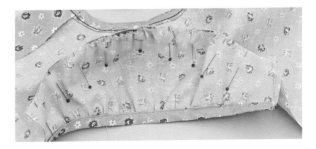

FRONT

BACK

Connecting the Sleeves and Sides

Follow Steps 1 and 2 for the Charlotte Dress (Connecting the Sleeves and Sides, page 24) to connect the sleeves and sides.

Finishing the Blouse

1. Sew the hem (see Sewing a Hem, page 15).

2. Make 5–7 buttonholes, depending on your chosen size, on the right-hand center back edge of the blouse. Center the buttonholes on the double layer of fabric. Place the first buttonhole ½″ down from the neck and space the remaining buttonholes evenly (see Making Buttonholes, page 12). Sew the buttons on the opposite back edge. Or, attach the snaps.

LEANNA BLOUSE INSPIRATION

Thelma
DRESS AND BLOUSE

SKILL LEVEL: Intermediate *** | SIZE: 12 months–5 years

A cute dress and blouse set with unique gathers on the front, the Thelma Dress and Blouse is an all-around, multipurpose pattern. The collar of the pattern can be made with the same fabric as the body or a different, coordinating one. Dresses like this one work perfectly for formal or casual outings. Match the Thelma Blouse with shorts or leggings for a great combination.

MATERIALS FOR DRESS/BLOUSE

Dress:

- 1¾ yards 44˝-wide fabric or 1⅝ yards 58˝-wide fabric for dress

- ¼ yard 44˝-wide or 58˝-wide fabric for lining

Blouse:

- 1¼ yards 44˝-wide fabric or 1 yard 58˝-wide fabric for blouse

- ¼ yard 44˝-wide or 58˝-wide fabric for lining

For either:

- ¼ yard or 1 fat quarter for contrast collar (*optional*)

- ¼ yard lightweight fusible interfacing for collar (*optional*)

- 2 buttons (½˝ / 12mm) or snaps

CUTTING FOR DRESS/BLOUSE

Trace each pattern piece in the desired size and transfer any markings (see Tracing the Patterns, page 8). Cut out the pieces, referring to the appropriate cutting layout. Optional: Finish the front, back, sleeve, front bottom, and back bottom seams in advance (see Finishing Seams, page 9).

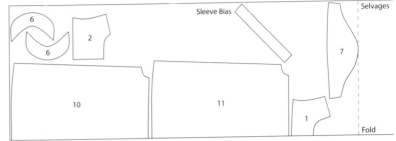

44˝-wide fabric suggested cutting layout for dress

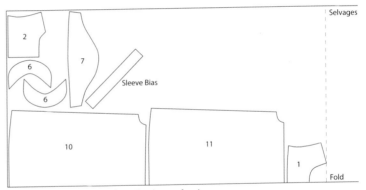

58˝-wide fabric suggested cutting layout for dress

Dress/blouse fabric

- Cut 1 Front 1 on fold (short).

- Cut 2 Back 2 (short).

- Cut 1 Front Bottom 10 on fold (dress: long; blouse: short).

- Cut 1 Back Bottom 11 on fold (dress: long; blouse: short).

- Cut 2 Sleeve 7 (short).

- Cut 2 bias strips for sleeve trim 1¾˝ wide by the length listed for the size you've chosen:

12 mos:	9½˝
18 mos:	9¾˝
24 mos:	10˝
3 yrs:	10¼˝
4 yrs:	10½˝
5 yrs:	10¾˝

- *If matching collar:* Cut 4 Collar 6 (*optional*).

Lining fabric

- Cut 1 Front 1 on fold (short).

- Cut 2 Back 2 (short).

Contrast collar fabric

- Cut 4 Collar 6 (*optional*).

Interfacing

- Cut 2 Collar 6 (*optional*).

- Read through all the project instructions before beginning to sew.

- A ⅜″ seam allowance is included on the pattern.

- A 1¾″ hem is included on the pattern.

- Backstitch at the beginning and end of each seam.

- Press after sewing each seam. Finish seams as desired.

Making the Collar

Follow Steps 1–5 for the Charlotte Dress (Making the Collar, page 20) to make the collar.

Make 2.

Assembling the Bodice and Lining

1. Follow Steps 1–8 for the Charlotte Dress (Assembling the Bodice and Lining, pages 21–23) to assemble the bodice and lining.

2. With the bodice right side out, overlap the left-hand back piece over the right, making sure the arm openings are aligned. Pin and baste the overlapped back pieces together at the bottom.

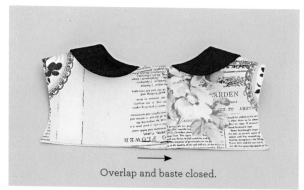

Overlap and baste closed.

Making and Attaching the Bottom

1. Gather the top edge of the bottom front piece (see Making Gathers, page 14).

2. Pin the bottom front piece and the front of the lined bodice, right sides together, at the side seams. Adjust the gathers to fit and then pin the rest.

3. Stitch the bottom front piece and lined bodice front together.

4. Repeat Steps 1–3 to make and attach the bottom back piece to the bodice.

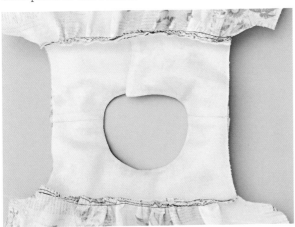

FRONT

BACK

Making and Attaching the Sleeves

Follow Steps 1–9 for the Charlotte Dress (Making and Attaching the Sleeves, pages 23 and 24) to make and attach the sleeves.

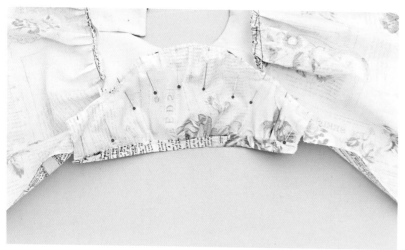

Connecting the Sleeves and Sides

Follow Step 1 for the Charlotte Dress (Connecting the Sleeves and Sides, page 24) to connect the sleeves and sides.

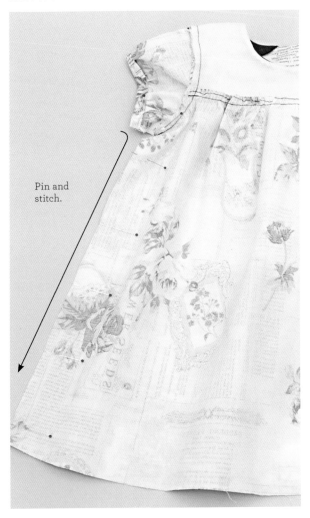

Pin and stitch.

Finishing the Dress or Blouse

1. Sew the hem (see Sewing a Hem, page 15).

2. Make 2 buttonholes on the bodice back (see Making Buttonholes, page 12, and Charlotte Dress, Finishing the Dress, page 24). Sew on the buttons. Or, attach the snaps.

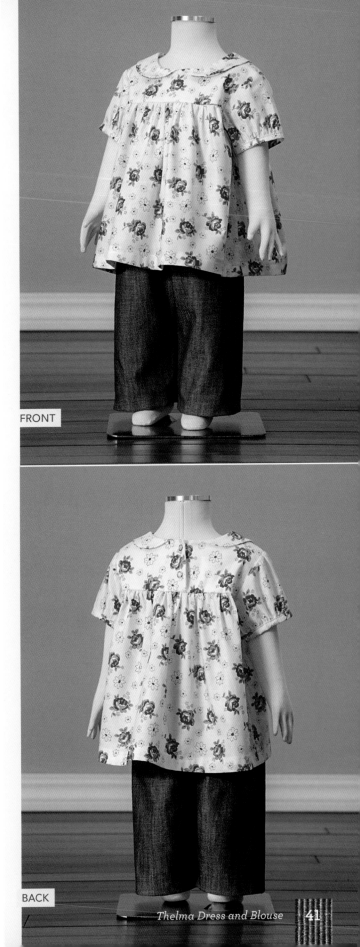

FRONT

BACK

THELMA DRESS AND BLOUSE INSPIRATION

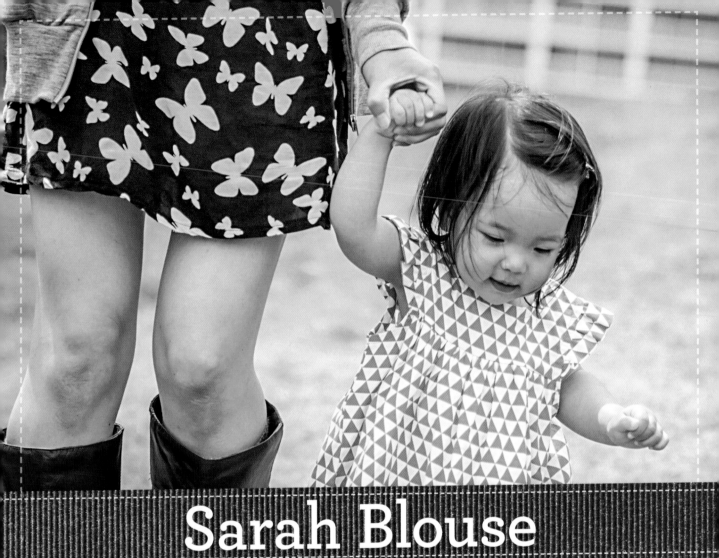

Sarah Blouse

SKILL LEVEL: Intermediate ✱✱✱　|　SIZE: 12 months–5 years

The cap sleeves perfectly define the Sarah Blouse and allow for movement and extra cooling during the summer. It is perfect to wear with pants, shorts, or leggings, or as a pinafore apron over a dress—a fashionable look for any outing!

MATERIALS

- 1 yard 44˝-wide or 58˝-wide fabric for blouse
- 2–4 buttons (½˝ / 12mm) or snaps

CUTTING

Trace each pattern piece in the desired size and transfer any markings (see Tracing the Patterns, page 8). On the Back 2 pattern piece, trace the extended center back line (see the Leanna Blouse, Cutting, page 31). Cut out the pieces, referring to the appropriate cutting layout. Optional: Finish the front, back, front bottom, and back bottom seams in advance (see Finishing Seams, page 9).

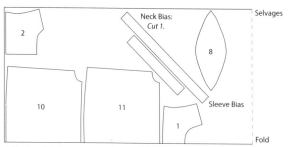

44˝-wide fabric suggested cutting layout

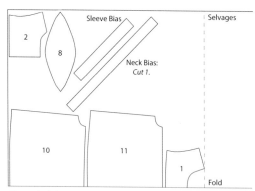

58˝-wide fabric suggested cutting layout

Blouse fabric

- Cut 1 Front 1 (short) on fold.
- Cut 2 Back 2 (short).
- Cut 1 Front Bottom 10 (short) on fold.
- Cut 1 Back Bottom 11 (short) on fold.
- Cut 2 Sleeve 8.
- Cut 1 bias strip for neckline trim 1¾˝ × 19½˝.
- Cut 2 bias strips for sleeve trim 1¾˝ wide by the length listed for the size you've chosen.

  12 mos: 14˝

  18 mos: 14½˝

  24 mos: 15˝

  3 yrs: 15⅝˝

  4 yrs: 16⅛˝

  5 yrs: 16⅝˝

You do not need to press any of these bias strips in advance.

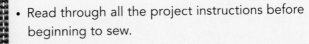

- Read through all the project instructions before beginning to sew.
- A ⅜˝ seam allowance is included on the pattern.
- A 1¾˝ hem is included on the pattern.
- Backstitch at the beginning and end of each seam.
- Press after sewing each seam. Finish seams as desired.

Assembling the Front and Back

1. Follow Steps 1–9 for the Leanna Blouse (Assembling the Front and Back, page 32) to assemble the front and back.

2. Turn the bodice right side out. Follow Step 2 for the Thelma Dress (Assembling the Bodice and Lining, page 38) to baste the overlapped back pieces together at the bottom.

Making and Attaching the Bottom

Follow Steps 1–4 for the Thelma Dress (Making and Attaching the Bottom, page 39) to attach the front and back bottom pieces.

Making the Sleeves

1. Fold a sleeve in half, *wrong sides together*, and press.

2. See Making Gathers (page 14) to gather both layers of the sleeve along the curved raw edges. *Figures A and B*

3. Pin the sleeve to the right side of the partially assembled top, pinning the sleeve at each end to the bodice seam. Adjust the gathers and baste the sleeve to the bodice. *Figure C*

4. Pin the armhole bias strip in place around the entire armhole, from the top corner of the back bottom piece to the top corner of the front bottom piece, aligning the raw edges. *Figure D*

5. Stitch all along the bias strip with a ⅜˝ seam allowance. Cut off any excess bias tape. Notch the curved seam. *Figure E*

6. Fold the bias strip over to the blouse's wrong side. Press. *Figure F*

7. Fold the loose bias in half, tucking the raw edge under to the wrong side. Press again. *Figure G*

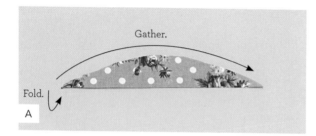

Gather.

Fold.

A

Folded edge

B

C

D

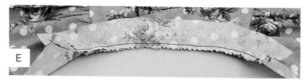

E

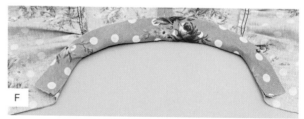

F

G

8. Pin and stitch all around the armhole. Repeat Steps 1–8 for the other armhole.

Connecting the Sleeves and Sides

Follow Step 1 for the Charlotte Dress (see Connecting the Sleeves and Sides, page 24) to connect the sides.

Pin and stitch.

Finishing the Blouse

1. Sew the hem (see Sewing a Hem, page 15).

2. Make 2–4 buttonholes (see Making Buttonholes, page 12, and Charlotte Dress, Finishing the Dress, page 24) on the back of the blouse. Sew on the buttons. Or, attach the snaps.

FRONT

BACK

SARAH BLOUSE INSPIRATION

Boutique Casual for Boys & Girls

Heidi
DRESS AND BLOUSE

SKILL LEVEL: Beginner * | SIZE: 12 months–5 years

Simple yet adorable, the Heidi Dress was designed to be suitable for all beginners. The dress is trimmed with bias binding, making the pattern more accessible than dresses with linings or collars. Matching the dress with a cardigan and a T-shirt makes a wonderful combination. It can be made using two or three gathered tiers, allowing the shorter dress to be worn with a pair of pants.

The blouse is a variation of the Heidi Dress with a single wide ruffle, utilizing adorable gathers as its feature character. Wear the blouse during the warm summer, or layer a cardigan over it when it gets a little chilly. Beneath it, wearing leggings and shorts or a variety of other clothing will look fashionable with this easy-to-coordinate design. Pin on a corsage for additional classy style.

MATERIALS FOR DRESS/BLOUSE

- 1¼ yards 44˝-wide fabric or ⅞ yard 58˝-wide fabric for dress
- 1 yard 44˝-wide fabric or ⅝ yard 58˝-wide fabric for blouse
- 2–3 buttons (½˝ / 12mm) or snaps

CUTTING FOR DRESS/BLOUSE

Trace each pattern piece in the desired size and transfer any markings (see Tracing the Patterns, page 8). Cut out the pieces, referring to the appropriate cutting layout. Optional: Finish the front, back, and skirt seams in advance (see Finishing Seams, page 9).

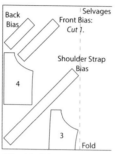

44˝-wide fabric suggested cutting layout for dress

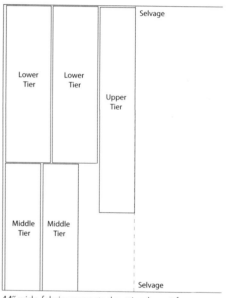

44˝-wide fabric suggested cutting layout for dress, continued

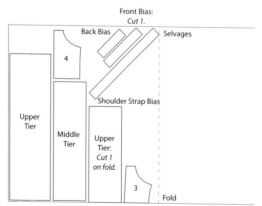

58˝-wide fabric suggested cutting layout for dress

Dress/blouse fabric

- Cut 1 Front 3 on fold.

- Cut 2 Back 4.

- *For the dress*, cut the rectangles listed for the skirt tiers for the size that you've chosen:

  12 mos: 4¾″ × 30¼″ (upper), 2 at 4¾″ × 18⅞″ (middle), and 2 at 6⅛″ × 23⅛″ (lower)

  18 mos: 5¼″ × 31½″, 2 at 5¼″ × 19⅝″, and 2 at 6⅝″ × 24″

  24 mos: 5¾″ × 32¾″, 2 at 5¾″ × 20⅜″, and 2 at 7⅛″ × 24⅜″

  3 yrs: 6¼″ × 34″, 2 at 6¼″ × 21⅛″, and 2 at 7⅝″ × 25⅞″

  4 yrs: 6¾″ × 35¼″, 2 at 6¾″ × 21⅞″, and 2 at 8⅛″ × 26⅞″

  5 yrs: 7¼″ × 36½″, 2 at 7¼″ × 22⅝″, and 2 at 8⅝″ × 27¾″

Optional: If you want a shorter dress, cut just the upper and middle tiers in your size.

- *For the blouse,* cut 1 rectangle for the ruffle in the size you've chosen:

  12 mos: 10⅛″ × 36½″

  18 mos: 10⅝″ × 37″

  24 mos: 11⅛″ × 37½″

  3 yrs: 11⅝″ × 38″

  4 yrs: 12⅛″ × 38½″

  5 yrs: 12⅝″ × 39″

- Cut the following bias strips 1½″ wide by the length listed for the size you've chosen:

SIZE	BODICE FRONT: CUT 1	BODICE BACK: CUT 2	SHOULDER STRAPS: CUT 2
12 Months	7½″	5″	14½″
18 Months	7⅝″	5⅛″	14¾″
24 Months	7¾″	5¼″	15″
3 Years	7⅞″	5⅜″	15⅜″
4 Years	8″	5½″	15⅝″
5 Years	8⅛″	5⅝″	15⅞″

- Read through all the project instructions before beginning to sew.

- A ⅜″ seam allowance is included on the pattern—sew with a ⅜″ seam allowance unless otherwise noted. A 1″ hem is included on the dress.

- Backstitch at the beginning and end of each seam.

- Press after sewing each seam. Finish seams as desired.

FRONT

BACK

Assembling the Bodice

1. Fold over the center back edge of both bodice back pieces ⅜″ to the wrong side and press. *Figure A*

2. On *just* the left-hand bodice back piece, fold and press an additional 1″ to the wrong side. *Figure B*

3. Fold and press all the bias strips to make double-fold bias tape (see Making Bias Strips, page 10). On both bodice back bias trim pieces, fold and press a short end in ¼″ to the wrong side. *Figure C*

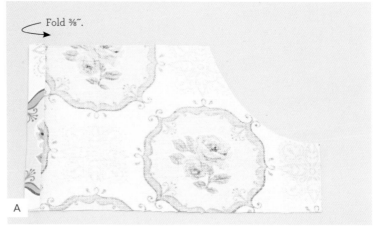

Fold ⅜″.

A

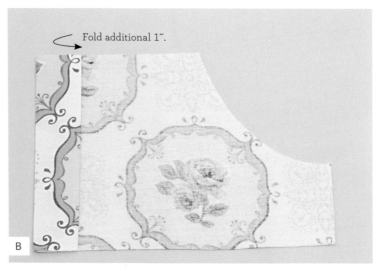

Fold additional 1″.

B

Fold short end in ¼″.

C

4. Matching the folded ends, encase the top of both bodice back pieces with the bias trim and pin in place. Edgestitch through all layers (see Trimming with Bias Strips, page 11). *Figure D*

5. Repeat Step 4 on the bodice front. Trim any excess bias from the bodice. *Figure E*

6. Pin the bodice front and back pieces right sides together as shown, aligning the raw edges at the sides and bottoms. Sew the side seams. *Figure F*

7. Open out the folds on a shoulder strap bias strip and sew the short ends, right sides together, to make a loop. Repeat with the remaining bias strip. *Figure G*

8. Fold the loops back into the pressed folds. Encase the lower armhole with the double-fold bias trim loop, matching the seams at the side, and pin it in place on the bodice. Edgestitch the bias trim to the bodice and then continue to stitch all the way around the loop. This will finish the armhole and make the shoulder strap all together. *Figure H*

Sew the remaining bias loop to the other side in the same manner.

G

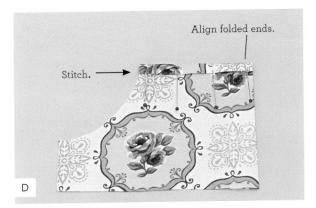

Align folded ends.

Stitch.

D

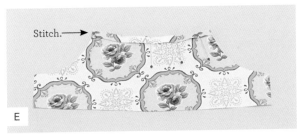

Stitch.

E

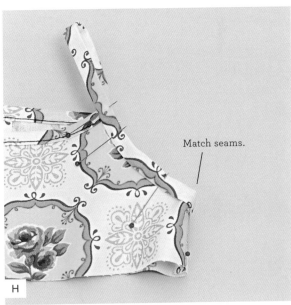

Match seams.

H

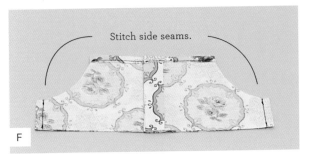

Stitch side seams.

F

FRONT

BACK

Making and Attaching the Skirt/Ruffle

Follow Steps 1–6 for the Maria Dress (Making and Attaching the Skirt, pages 27 and 28) to make the tiered skirt or blouse ruffle and attach it to the bodice.

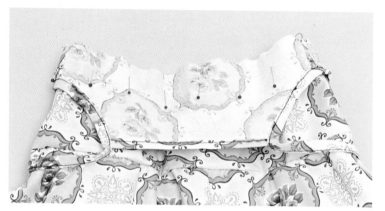

Finishing the Dress/Blouse

1. Sew the hem, folding ½″ to the wrong side twice (see Sewing a Hem, page 15).

2. Make 2–3 buttonholes on the bodice back (see Making Buttonholes, page 12, and Charlotte Dress, Finishing the Dress, page 24). Sew on the buttons. Or, attach the snaps.

HEIDI DRESS AND BLOUSE INSPIRATION

Ranger Cargo
PANTS AND SHORTS

SKILL LEVEL: Intermediate *** | Size: 12 months–5 years

Boutique Casual for Boys & Girls

These cargo pants have pockets on the front, back, and sides, allowing for lots of storage room. They can be worn as activewear for both boys and girls. The pants have two front patch pockets, two back patch pockets, and two side cargo pockets. For the shorts, it is best to omit all the upper pockets and make only the cargo pockets.

The design and the elastic band allow children to wear the pants comfortably when running around or being active. The pattern works great with cotton, denim, or single knit fabrics.

MATERIALS FOR PANTS/SHORTS

- 1⅛ yards 44″-wide fabric or ⅞ yard 58″-wide fabric for pants

- ⅞ yard 44″-wide fabric or ⅝ yard 58″-wide fabric for shorts

- 4 buttons (¾″ / 18mm) or snaps

- 1 yard of 1″-wide elastic

CUTTING FOR PANTS/SHORTS

Trace each pattern piece in the desired size and transfer any markings (see Tracing the Patterns, page 8). Cut out the pieces, referring to the appropriate cutting layout. Optional: *Finish the front and back seams in advance (see Finishing Seams, page 9).*

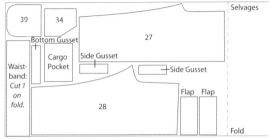

44″-wide fabric suggested cutting layout for pants

Pants/shorts fabric

- Cut 2 Front 27 (pants: long; shorts: medium).

- Cut 2 Back 28 (pants: long; shorts: medium).

- Cut 2 Front Patch Pocket 34 (pants only).

- Cut 2 Back Patch Pocket 39 (pants only).

- Cut 1 rectangle for the waistband in the size you've chosen:

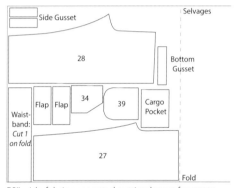

58″-wide fabric suggested cutting layout for pants

- Cut 2 rectangles for the cargo pocket in the size you've chosen:

12 mos: 4″ × 26″	12 mos: 5¼″ × 3¾″
18 mos: 4″ × 27″	18 mos: 5⅜″ × 3⅞″
24 mos: 4″ × 28″	24 mos: 5½″ × 4″
3 yrs: 4″ × 29″	3 yrs: 6″ × 4½″
4 yrs: 4″ × 30″	4 yrs: 6⅛″ × 4⅝″
5 yrs: 4″ × 31″	5 yrs: 6¼″ × 4¾″

- Cut 4 rectangles for the cargo pocket flap in the size you've chosen:

  12 mos: 5¼˝ × 2⅜˝

  18 mos: 5⅜˝ × 2⅜˝

  24 mos: 5½˝ × 2⅜˝

  3 yrs: 6˝ × 2⅞˝

  4 yrs: 6⅛˝ × 2⅞˝

  5 yrs: 6¼˝ × 2⅞˝

- Cut 4 rectangles for the cargo pocket side gussets in the size you've chosen:

  12 mos: 1½˝ × 3¾˝

  18 mos: 1½˝ × 3⅞˝

  24 mos: 1½˝ × 4˝

  3 yrs: 1½˝ × 4½˝

  4 yrs: 1½˝ × 4⅝˝

  5 yrs: 1½˝ × 4¾˝

- Cut 2 rectangles for the cargo pocket bottom gussets in the size you've chosen:

  12 mos: 5¼˝ × 1½˝

  18 mos: 5⅜˝ × 1½˝

  24 mos: 5½˝ × 1½˝

  3 yrs: 6˝ × 1½˝

  4 yrs: 6⅛˝ × 1½˝

  5 yrs: 6¼˝ × 1½˝

- Read through all the project instructions before beginning to sew.
- A ⅜˝ seam allowance is included on the pattern.
- A 1¾˝ hem is included on the pattern.
- Backstitch at the beginning and end of each seam.
- Press after sewing each seam. Finish seams as desired.

Making and Attaching the Front Patch Pockets (Pants Only)

1. Fold both sides and the bottom of the front patch pockets over ⅜˝ to the wrong side and press. *Figure A*

2. Topstitch ⅛˝ and ¼˝ from the edge of the pockets along the angled edge only. *Figure B*

3. Aligning the raw edges at the top and the short side, pin the pockets to the pants front pieces, both right sides up. Sew the pockets to the pants in an L shape by stitching ⅛˝ and ¼˝ from both the straight side and the bottom, pivoting at the corner. *Figure C*

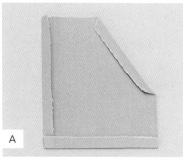

A

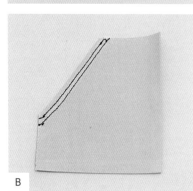

B

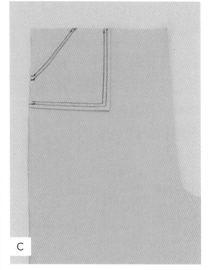

C

Making the Casing and Attaching the Waistband

1. To make the elastic casing, fold the waistband in half lengthwise, wrong sides together, and press. Then, fold over the long sides of the waistband ⅜˝ toward the wrong side and press. *Figure A*

2. Open out the folds and align the short ends. Pin and sew the short ends to make a loop. Press the seam open. *Figure B*

3. Pin the waistband to the top of the pants, right sides together, aligning the raw edges and the seams at the center back. Pin and sew all around. *Figure C*

4. Press the waistband up and away from the pants. Fold the waistband in half again toward the wrong side along the center pressed line, making sure the pressed edge at the bottom of the waistband will cover your previous line of stitching. Pin in place. *Figure D*

5. Edgestitch the bottom of the waistband, leaving a 2˝ opening at the back to insert the elastic. Edgestitch through both layers at the top of the waistband. *Figure E*

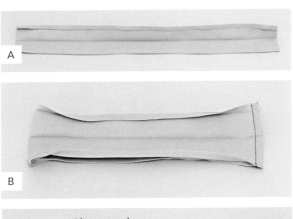

A

B

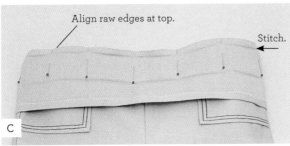

Align raw edges at top.

Stitch.

C

Fold waistband over to wrong side.

D

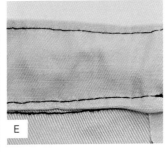

E

Inserting the Elastic

1. Refer to the elastic size chart on page 12 to cut a piece of the 1˝-wide elastic to the correct length for the size you have chosen.

2. Insert the elastic, stitch the ends, and close up the casing (see Inserting Elastic into a Casing, page 13).

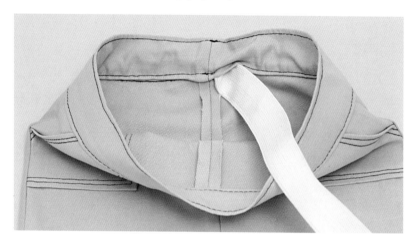

Finishing the Pants/Shorts

1. Sew the hem (see Sewing a Hem, page 15).

2. Sew a button to each corner of the cargo pocket flap for decorative use only. *Optional:* Make buttonholes in the cargo pocket flap (see Making Buttonholes, page 12) and sew the buttons to the cargo pocket itself.

Cropped
PANTS WITH CUFFS

SKILL LEVEL: Beginner * | SIZE: 12 months–5 years

The Cropped Pants with Cuffs bring you an easy-to-make pair of pants for your little boy or girl. With two back pockets, different-colored cuffs, and an elastic waistband, this pair of pants is not only cute, it's also extra comfy! Great for indoor or outdoor wear, the Cropped Pants will become one of your child's favorite pairs of pants.

MATERIALS

- 1 yard 44˝- to 58˝-wide lightweight or quilting-weight cotton fabric for pants

- ¼ yard 44˝- to 58˝-wide lightweight or quilting-weight cotton fabric for waistband and cuffs

- 1 yard 1˝-wide elastic

CUTTING

Trace the cuff patterns first in your desired size (see Tracing the Patterns, page 8). Then place the cuff patterns on top of the corresponding pant patterns, find where the side seams match perfectly at the tops of the cuff patterns, and trace the cuff patterns onto the pants leg patterns. Cut out new pants leg patterns just for the Cropped Pants.

Cut out the pieces, referring to the cutting layouts. Optional: Finish the front, back, front cuff, and back cuff seams in advance (see Finishing Seams, page 9).

44˝- and 58˝-wide pants fabric suggested cutting layout

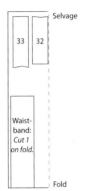

44˝- and 58˝-wide contrast fabric suggested cutting layout

Pants fabric

- Cut 2 Front 27 (long).

- Cut 2 Back 28 (long).

- Cut 2 Front Patch Pocket 34 (*optional*).

- Cut 4 Back Patch Pocket 39 (*optional*).

Waistband/cuff fabric

- Cut 1 rectangle for the waistband in the size you've chosen:

  - 12 mos: 4˝ × 26˝

  - 18 mos: 4˝ × 27˝

  - 24 mos: 4˝ × 28˝

  - 3 yrs: 4˝ × 29˝

  - 4 yrs: 4˝ × 30˝

  - 5 yrs: 4˝ × 31˝

- Cut 2 Front Cuff 32.

- Cut 2 Back Cuff 33.

- Read through all the project instructions before beginning to sew.

- A ⅜″ seam allowance is included on the pattern.

- Backstitch at the beginning and end of each seam.

- Press after sewing each seam. Finish seams as desired.

Making and Attaching the Pockets (optional)

1. Follow Steps 1–3 for the Ranger Cargo Pants (Making and Attaching the Front Patch Pockets, page 58) to make and attach the front pockets.

2. Follow Steps 1–4 for the Ranger Cargo Pants (Making and Attaching the Back Patch Pockets, page 59) to make and attach the back pockets.

Assembling the Pants

1. Pin the pants front and pants back pieces, right sides together, along the straight side. Stitch the side seam. Press the seam open.

2. Follow Steps 1–3 for the Ranger Cargo Pants (Assembling the Pants/Shorts, page 62) to continue assembling the pants.

Making the Casing and Attaching the Waistband

Follow Steps 1–5 for the Ranger Cargo Pants (Making the Casing and Attaching the Waistband, page 63) to make the casing and attach the waistband.

Inserting the Elastic

1. Refer to the elastic size chart on page 12 to cut a piece of the 1"-wide elastic to the correct length for the size you have chosen.

2. Insert the elastic, stitch the ends, and close up the casing (see Inserting Elastic into a Casing, page 13).

Adding the Cuffs

1. Pin a front cuff and a back cuff right sides together, matching the short ends (straight sides together and angled sides together). Sew along the short ends. Repeat to sew the other cuff pieces. Press side seams open.

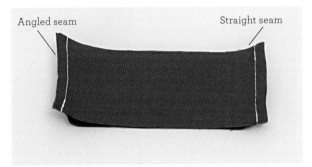

Angled seam   Straight seam

2. Tuck a pant leg into an assembled cuff, right sides together. Align the raw edges at the bottom and make sure the side seams match. The straight seam on the cuff should be matched to the straight side seam of the pant leg. Pin and sew together. Repeat this step on the other pant leg.

Angled side of cuff

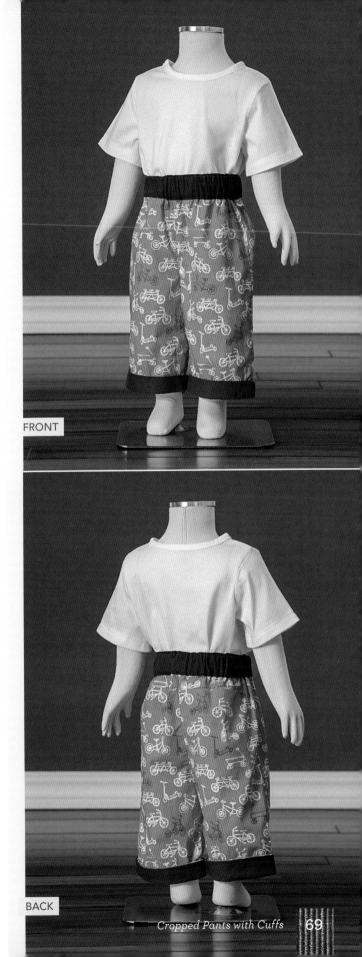

FRONT

BACK

3. Turn the cuffs to the inside of the pants legs. Press the seams flat.

4. Turn the pants inside out so the pants legs and cuffs are wrong sides together. Stitch ⅜˝ from the raw edge of each cuff all around through both layers.

5. Turn the pants right side out and fold the cuffs up. Press the cuffs.

CROPPED PANTS WITH CUFFS INSPIRATION

Girl's Shorts
BLOOMER STYLE

SKILL LEVEL: Beginner * | **SIZE:** 12 months–5 years

By adding elastic to the leg opening of a basic shorts pattern, you can make an effective bloomer for girls! They can be worn under a dress or as shorts for the summer. Beginning sewists should be able to make these in no time.

MATERIALS

- ¾ yard 44″- or 58″-wide fabric for bloomers

- 1 yard of 1″-wide elastic for waistband

- ½ yard of ½″-wide elastic for leg openings

CUTTING

Trace each pattern piece in the desired size and transfer any markings (see Tracing the Patterns, page 8).

Extend the waist up 3⅝″ on the pants front and pants back. Trace each piece only down to the "short" line on the pattern and be sure to trace the folded hem allowance at the side for the bloomers..

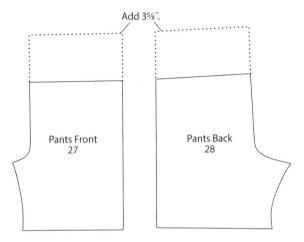

Cut out the pieces, referring to the appropriate cutting layout. Optional: *Finish the front and back seams in advance (see Finishing Seams, page 9).*

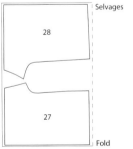

44″- and 58″-wide fabric cutting layout for bloomers

Bloomer fabric

- Cut 2 Front 27 (short).

- Cut 2 Back 28 (short).

- Read through all the project instructions before beginning to sew.

- A ⅜″ seam allowance is included on the pattern.

- Backstitch at the beginning and end of each seam.

- Press after sewing each seam. Finish seams as desired.

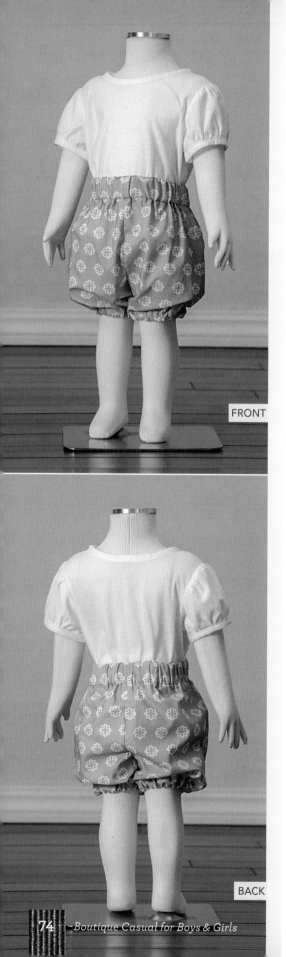

Assembling the Bloomers

1. Pin the pants front and pants back pieces, right sides together, along the straight side. Stitch the side seam. Press the seam open.

2. See Steps 1–3 for the Ranger Cargo Pants (Assembling the Pants/Shorts, page 62) to continue assembling the bloomers.

Making the Casing

Assemble the casing (see Making the Casing, page 13) for the waist elastic.

Finishing the Bloomers

Sew a ⅞″ double-fold hem (see Sewing a Hem, page 15), leaving a small opening at the back of each leg for the elastic. *Figure A*

Inserting the Elastic

1. Refer to the elastic size chart on page 12 to cut a piece of the 1″-wide elastic to the correct waist length for the size you have chosen and 2 pieces of the ½″-wide elastic to the correct thigh length for the size you have chosen.

2. Insert the elastic into the waist and leg openings, stitch the ends, and close up the casings (see Inserting Elastic into a Casing, page 13). *Figure B*

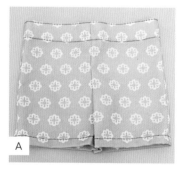

A

B

GIRL'S SHORTS—BLOOMER STYLE INSPIRATION

Double-Button
HOODED JACKET

SKILL LEVEL: Confident Beginner ★★ | **SIZE:** 12 months–5 years

The Double-Button Hooded Jacket is a stylish jacket for your baby to wear on those breezy spring or autumn days. Using a knit or jersey fabric lining will make it especially warm and soft. The hood is designed to keep warm air circulating around your child's head and face. The Double-Button Hooded Jacket is quite easy to sew and makes a wonderful personal gift. This simple-but-cute unisex jacket is great with all outfits, from dresses and flats to pants and rain boots.

MATERIALS

- 1⅝ yards 44″-wide fabric or 1⅛ yards 58″-wide fabric for jacket

- 1⅝ yards 44″-wide fabric or 1⅛ yards 58″-wide fabric for lining

- 8 buttons (¾″/18mm– 20mm) or snaps

- 1 sew-on hook and eye

CUTTING

Trace each pattern piece in the desired size and transfer any markings (see Tracing the Patterns, page 8). **Make sure to follow the directions on the Jacket Front 40 piece to trace the correct neckline.** *Cut out the pieces, referring to the appropriate cutting layout. You don't need to finish the seams, since the jacket is fully lined.*

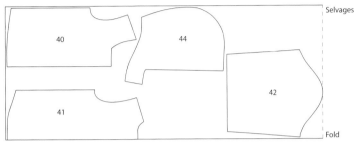

44″-wide fabric suggested cutting layout for jacket and lining

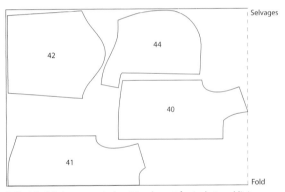

58″-wide fabric suggested cutting layout for jacket and lining

Jacket fabric

- Cut 2 Jacket Front 40.

- Cut 1 Jacket Back 41 on fold.

- Cut 2 Sleeve 42.

- Cut 2 Hood 44.

Lining fabric

- Cut 2 Jacket Front 40.

- Cut 1 Jacket Back 41 on fold.

- Cut 2 Sleeve 42.

- Cut 2 Hood 44.

- Read through all the project instructions before beginning to sew.

- A ⅜″ seam allowance is included on the pattern—sew with a ⅜″ seam allowance unless otherwise noted.

- Backstitch at the beginning and end of each seam.

- Press after sewing each seam. Finish seams as desired.

Making the Hood

1. Pin the 2 jacket hood pieces, right sides together, along the curved outer edge, matching the notches. Sew the curved edge. *Figure A*

2. Notch the curved portion of the seam. Press the seam open. *Figure B*

3. Repeat Steps 1 and 2 to make the hood lining.

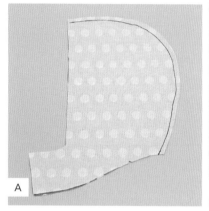

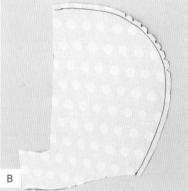

Making the Jacket Body and Lining

1. Align both jacket front pieces with the jacket back at the shoulders, right sides together. Pin and sew the fronts to the back piece along the shoulder seams. Press the seams open. *Figure A*

2. Pin the top of the sleeve to the jacket at the armhole, right sides together. Pin the center and end points first, and then pin the rest, easing the fabric as needed. Sew the sleeve to the front and back. *Figure B*

3. Clip the curved seam. Press.

4. Repeat Steps 1–3 to attach the other sleeve in the same manner.

5. Fold the jacket body, right sides together, at the shoulders, aligning the raw edges of the sleeves and the side seams of the front and back pieces. Pin and sew, starting at the bottom of the sleeve, all the way to the jacket hem, pivoting where the sleeve meets the body. *Figure C*

6. Repeat Step 5 to sew the other sleeve/side seam.

7. Pin the hood to the assembled jacket, right sides together. Sew along the neckline. Clip the curved seams. *Figure D*

8. Repeat Steps 1–7 to assemble the lining body. Leave an opening in a side seam for turning.

B

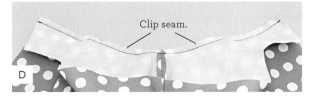

Clip seam.

D

Assembling the Jacket and Lining

1. Turn the lining right side out.

2. Place the lining inside the wrong-side-out jacket so they are right sides together, matching the shoulder and side seams. Tuck the lining sleeves into the jacket sleeves.

3. Pin and sew around the perimeter of the jacket/lining—the hood, the left and right fronts, and the hem—dropping the sewing machine needle to pivot at each corner. *Figure A*

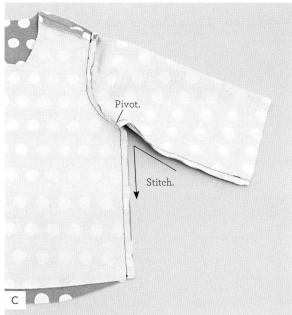

Pivot.

Stitch.

C

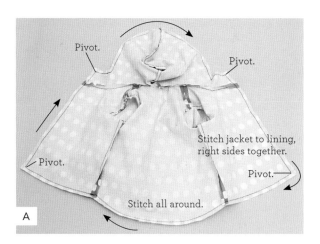

Pivot.

Pivot.

Pivot.

Stitch jacket to lining, right sides together.

Pivot.

Stitch all around.

A

4. Pull the sleeve lining out of and away from just *1* jacket sleeve. *Figure B*

5. Pin the sleeve lining to the jacket sleeve, right sides together and matching the sleeve seams, all around the sleeve. Make sure the lining is not twisted. *Figure C*

6. Sew the jacket and lining sleeve together at the hem, taking care not to catch any part of the

fabric as you stitch. Go slowly, turning the pinned-together lining and sleeve as you work around the circumference. *Figure D*

7. Repeat Steps 4–6 to finish the other sleeve.

8. Trim the corner seams. *Figure E*

9. Notch the intersecting seams. *Figure F*

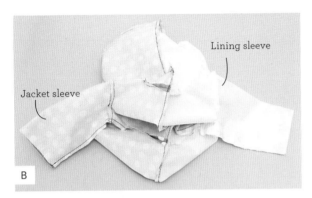

Jacket sleeve

Lining sleeve

B

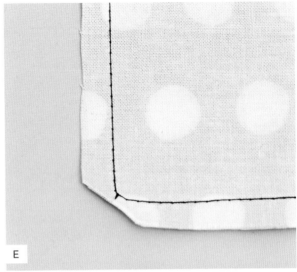

E

C

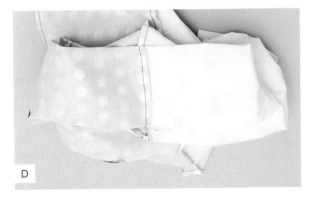

D

F

10. Turn the jacket right side out through the side opening. Pull the lining away from the jacket body, finger-press the seam allowances inside the opening, and topstitch it closed.

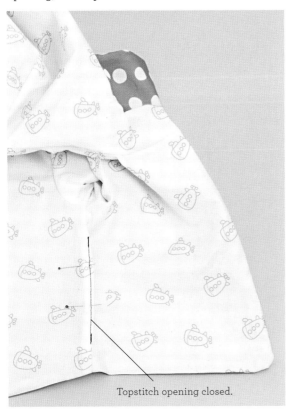
Topstitch opening closed.

11. Press the jacket. Spread out the jacket; pin and edgestitch around the outer seams, ⅛˝ from the seam. Press and edgestitch around the cuffs.

Finishing the Jacket

1. Make a row of 4 buttonholes ¼˝ from the edge of the jacket (see Making Buttonholes, page 12). Place the first buttonhole ¾˝ down from the hood seam, and space the remaining buttonholes evenly. Sew 4 buttons in a column 1¾˝ from the buttonholes (these are decorative buttons). Sew the remaining 4 buttons to the layer underneath. Or, attach the snaps.

2. Hand sew the hook and eye onto the top edge of the hood flaps where they overlap.

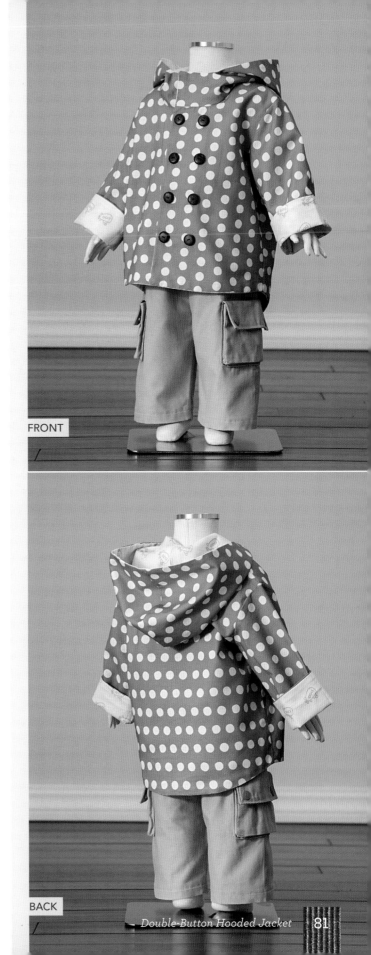
FRONT

BACK

DOUBLE-BUTTON HOODED JACKET INSPIRATION

Basic Jacket

SKILL LEVEL: Confident Beginner ** | SIZE: 12 months–5 years

The Basic Jacket includes a plain collar for a classic style. The basic design of the jacket allows it to coordinate with outfits for both boys and girls. The process of making this jacket is almost identical to making the Double-Button Hooded Jacket (page 76), but a collar replaces the hood for a more formal style. When this jacket is made with solid colors, it coordinates well with the majority of outfits, from pants to skirts. Since the sleeves show off the lining, choose your fabrics carefully.

CUTTING

*Trace each pattern piece in the desired size and transfer any markings (see Tracing the Patterns, page 8). **Make sure to follow the directions on the Jacket Front 40 piece to trace the correct neckline.** Cut out the pieces, referring to the appropriate cutting layout. You don't need to finish the seams, since this jacket is fully lined.*

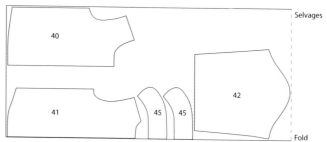

44″-wide fabric cutting layout for jacket

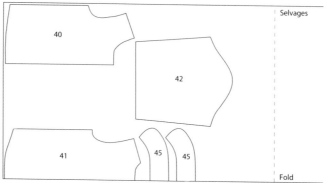

58″-wide fabric cutting layout for jacket

MATERIALS

- 1¼ yards 44″-wide fabric or 1⅛ yards 58″-wide fabric for jacket

- 1⅛ yards 44″- or 58″-wide fabric for lining

- ¼ yard of lightweight fusible interfacing for collar (*optional*)

- 4 buttons (1″–1¼″ / 25mm–30mm)

Jacket fabric

- Cut 2 Jacket Front 40.

- Cut 1 Jacket Back 41 on fold.

- Cut 2 Sleeve 42.

- Cut 2 Collar 45 on fold.

Lining fabric

- Cut 2 Jacket Front 40.

- Cut 1 Jacket Back 41 on fold.

- Cut 2 Sleeve 42.

Interfacing

- Cut 1 Collar 45 on fold (*optional*).

- Read through all the project instructions before beginning to sew.
- A ⅜″ seam allowance is included on the pattern.
- Backstitch at the beginning and end of each seam.
- Press after sewing each seam.

Making the Collar

1. Follow Steps 1–4 for the Charlotte Dress (Making the Collar, page 20) to make the collar.

2. Topstitch ⅛″ from the outer edge (*optional*).

Making the Jacket Body and Lining

1. Follow Steps 1–8 for the Double-Button Hooded Jacket (Making the Jacket Body and Lining, pages 78 and 79) to make the jacket and lining.

2. Pin the collar and the jacket body, right sides together, at the neckline, matching notches. Sew along the neckline. Clip the curved seam allowances.

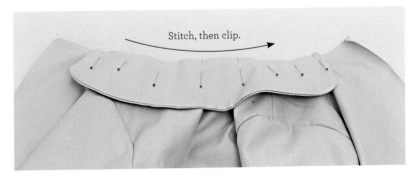

Stitch, then clip.

FRONT

BACK

Assembling the Jacket and Lining

Follow Steps 1–11 for the Double-Button Hooded Jacket (Assembling the Jacket and Lining, page 79) to assemble the jacket and lining.

Finishing the Jacket

Make 4 buttonholes on the jacket front (see Making Buttonholes, page 12). Place the first buttonhole ¼˝ in from the edge of the jacket front and ¾˝ down from the neckline edge. Space the remaining 3 buttonholes evenly. Sew on the buttons. Or, attach the snaps.

Multipurpose
HOODED SHIRT

SKILL LEVEL: Beginner * | SIZE: 12 months–5 years

This is a comfortable boxy hoodie that can be used in a variety of different situations. It can be a raincoat when made with waterproof fabric or a windbreaker if you use nylon; it also makes a great cover-up for the pool or beach if you use terry cloth. I'm sure you can think of a purpose for this hooded shirt using just about any fabric. This pattern is accessible to sewists of all levels!

MATERIALS

- 1⅝ yards 44″-wide fabric or 1⅓ yards 58″-wide fabric for shirt

- 4″ of ⅛″-wide elastic for button loop

- 1 button (1″ / 25mm)

CUTTING

Trace each pattern piece in the desired size and transfer any markings (see Tracing the Patterns, page 8). **Make sure to follow the directions on the Jacket Front 40 piece to trace the correct neckline and center front line. Extend the sleeve length 1⅝″ as shown, and add ⅝″ to the front and back hem.**

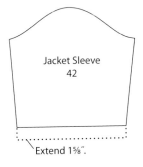
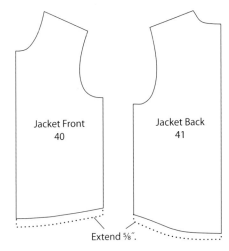

Jacket Sleeve 42

Extend 1⅝″.

Jacket Front 40

Jacket Back 41

Extend ⅝″.

Cut out the pieces, referring to the appropriate cutting layout, making sure to place the Jacket Front 40 piece **on the fold.** *Optional: Finish the front, back, sleeve, and hood seams in advance (see Finishing Seams, page 9).*

44″-wide fabric suggested cutting layout

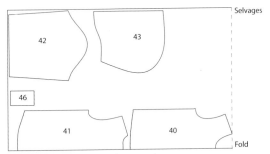

58″-wide fabric suggested cutting layout

Shirt fabric

- Cut 1 Jacket Front 40, placing the center front line on the fold.

- Cut 1 Jacket Back 41 on the fold.

- Cut 2 Sleeve 42.

- Cut 2 Hood 43.

- Cut 1 Front Facing 46.

- Read through all the project instructions before beginning to sew.

- A ⅜˝ seam allowance is included on the pattern.

- A 1˝ hem is included on the pattern.

- Backstitch at the beginning and end of each seam.

- Press after sewing each seam. Finish seams as desired.

Sewing the Front Opening

1. Fold the elastic in half. Pin it to the right side of the shirt front piece, centered and 1˝ down from the top. Stitch the loose ends of the elastic to the front piece. *Figure A*

2. Transfer the stitching line from the front facing pattern to the wrong side of the fabric. Pin the front facing and shirt front piece right sides together, centered, aligning the raw edges at the top. *Figure B*

3. Stitch on the opening line, pivoting at the corners. Cut a slit through both layers of fabric between the 2 lines of stitching. *Figure C*

4. Turn the facing to the wrong side and press. Edgestitch around the opening. *Figure D*

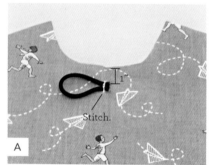

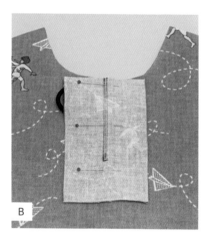

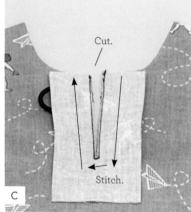

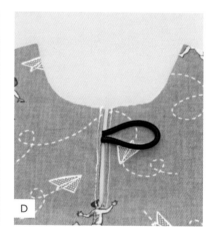

Making the Hood

1. Pin the hood pieces right sides together. Sew along the curved seam. Notch the seam allowances.

2. Fold the front of the hood (the straight edge) over ⅞″ to the wrong side and press. Fold and press another ⅞″. Edgestitch along the fold and press again.

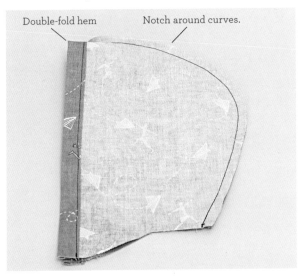

Double-fold hem   Notch around curves.

Making the Shirt and Adding the Hood

1. Pin the front and back pieces, right sides together, at the shoulders. Stitch both shoulder seams. Press the seams open.

2. Pin the hood to the shirt body, right sides together, aligning raw edges and matching notches to the shoulder seams. Stitch around the neckline.

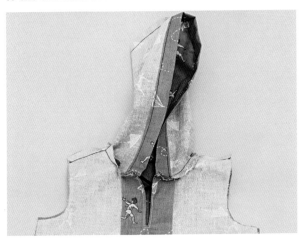

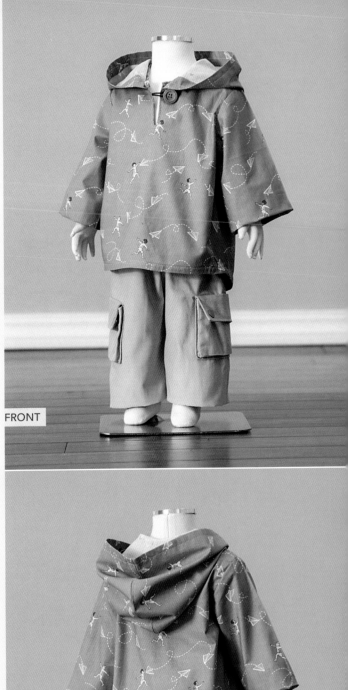

FRONT

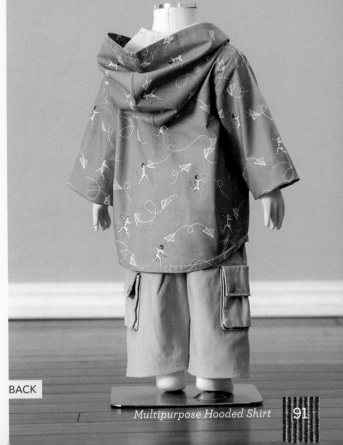

BACK

Connecting the Sleeves and Sides

Follow Steps 2–6 for the Double-Button Hooded Jacket (Making the Jacket Body and Lining, page 79) to sew the sleeves to the shirt at the shoulders and sew the shirt/side seams.

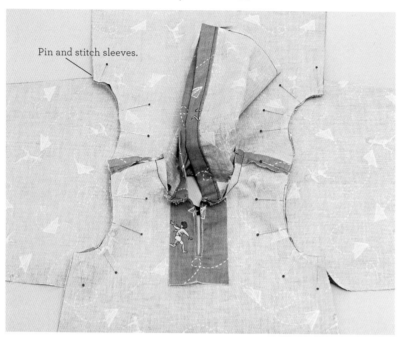

Pin and stitch sleeves.

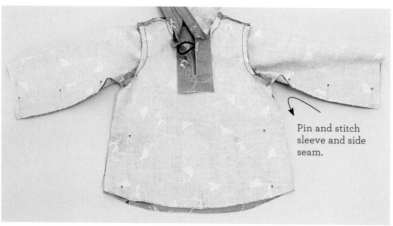

Pin and stitch sleeve and side seam.

Finishing the Shirt

Hem the sleeves and the shirt with ½˝ double-fold hems (see Sewing a Hem, page 15).

MULTIPURPOSE HOODED SHIRT INSPIRATION

Short-Sleeve T-Shirt

SKILL LEVEL: Confident Beginner ** | SIZE: 12 months–5 years

This is the most basic type of T-shirt, which can be used for almost any occasion. The Short-Sleeve T-Shirt is for boys and girls and can be worn throughout all four seasons—as an extra inner layer during cold weather and a simple shirt during warm weather. Using the optional puffed version of the sleeve, you can modify the look to be more girly. Consider recycling fabrics from old clothing instead of purchasing new ones. Be sure to use a single knit because you need the stretch of the fabric to get the shirt on and off. Sewing shirts in various colors will allow for easy coordination when choosing the perfect outfit for a day out!

MATERIALS

- 1⅛ yards 44˝- or 58˝-wide single knit fabric for shirt

- Sew-on patch (*optional*)

CUTTING

This shirt has no back closure, so you will need to alter the original Back pattern piece. Trace the Back 2 pattern piece in your desired size, but move the straight center back seam in ⅜˝ and trim away ¼˝ of the neckline. On the Front pattern piece, just trim away ¼˝ of the neckline. Trace either Sleeve 9 or Sleeve 7 as desired (see *Tracing the Patterns*, page 8). Cut out the pieces, referring to the appropriate cutting layout. You don't have to finish the seams, since knits are less likely to ravel than woven fabrics.

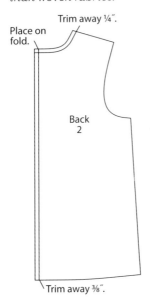

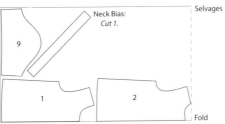

44˝-wide fabric cutting layout

58˝-wide fabric cutting layout

NOTE

Replace Sleeve 9 with the optional Sleeve 7 for all cutting layouts, if desired.

- - - - - - - - - - - - - - -

Shirt fabric

- Cut 1 Front 1 on fold (long).

- Cut 1 Back 2 on fold (long).

- Cut 2 Sleeve 9 (short).*

- Cut 1 bias strip for neckline trim 1¾˝ × 19½˝.

Alternative Puffed Sleeve Option:

- Cut 2 Sleeve 7 (short).

- Cut 2 bias strips for sleeve trim 1¾˝ wide by the length listed for the size you've chosen:

12 mos: 9½˝

18 mos: 9¾˝

24 mos: 10˝

3 yrs: 10¼˝

4 yrs: 10½˝

5 yrs: 10¾˝

- Read through all the project instructions before beginning to sew.

- A ⅜˝ seam allowance is included on the pattern.

- A 1˝ hem is included on the pattern.

- Refer to your sewing machine manual if you aren't sure of the best settings for sewing knits.

- Use a ball point or jersey needle.

- Backstitch at the beginning and end of each seam.

- Press after sewing each seam.

Assembling the Front and Back

1. Align the front and back pieces, right sides together, at *1* shoulder, matching the notches. Pin and stitch just the 1 shoulder seam together. Press the seam open. *Figure A*

2. Refer to Making Bias Strips (page 10) and Trimming with Bias Strips (page 11) to encase the neckline with the bias strip, beginning at the front shoulder. Pin in place. Stitch all around the neck. Cut off any excess bias trim. *Figure B*

3. Stitch the front and back pieces together at the other shoulder seam. *Figure C*

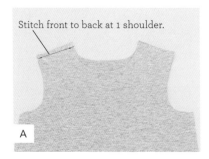

Stitch front to back at 1 shoulder.

A

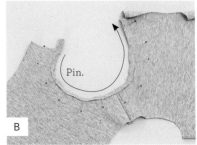

Pin.

B

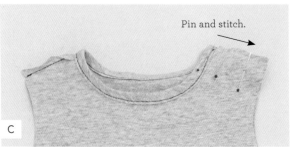

Pin and stitch.

C

Connecting the Sleeves and Sides

1. Follow Steps 2–4 for the Double-Button Hooded Jacket (Making the Jacket Body and Lining, page 79) to attach the sleeves to the shirt at the armholes.

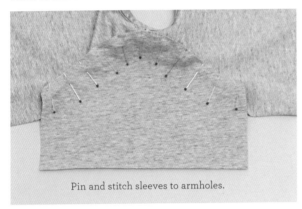

Pin and stitch sleeves to armholes.

NOTE

If you would like to add the optional puffed sleeve, follow Steps 1–9 for the Charlotte Dress (Making and Attaching the Sleeves, page 23).

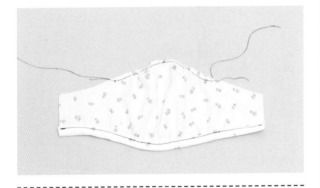

FRONT

BACK

2. Follow Steps 5 and 6 for the Double-Button Hooded Jacket (Making the Jacket Body and Lining, page 79) to stitch the side seams on the sleeves and shirt.

Pin and stitch sleeves and sides.

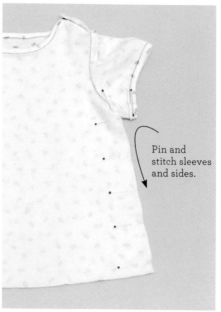
Pin and stitch sleeves and sides.

Finishing the Shirt

1. Sew the sleeve hem (see Sewing a Hem, page 15). Sew the shirt hem, but fold only ½˝ for each fold.

2. Attach the sew-on patch (*optional*).

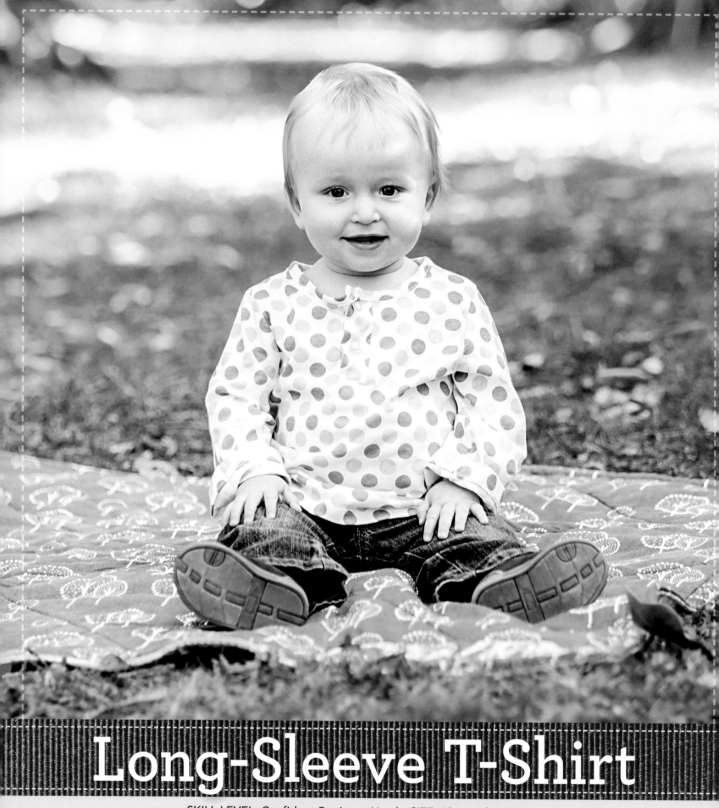

Long-Sleeve T-Shirt

SKILL LEVEL: Confident Beginner ** | SIZE: 12 months–5 years

*This Long-Sleeve T-Shirt
has a front opening
and is designed to fit
both boys and girls! It
is appropriate for many
occasions. Create several
shirts in different colors
so they can be matched
easily with other articles
of clothing. You can
also lend your personal
touch to it by adding an
embellishment. Be sure to
use a single knit because
you need the stretch of
the fabric for comfort.*

MATERIALS

- 1⅛ yards 44˝- or 58˝-wide
  single knit for shirt

- 2 buttons (⅜˝/10mm)
  or snaps

- ⅛ yard lightweight fusible
  interfacing

CUTTING

*Refer to the Short-Sleeve T-Shirt (page 94) to alter the original Front
and Back pattern pieces. Trace the pattern pieces in your desired size
(see Tracing the Patterns, page 8). Cut out the pieces, referring to the
appropriate cutting layout. You don't have to finish the seams, since
knits are less likely to ravel than woven fabrics.*

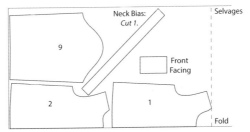

44˝-wide fabric cutting layout

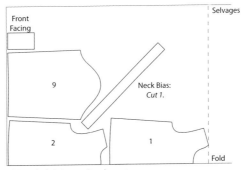

58˝-wide fabric cutting layout

Shirt fabric

- Cut 1 Front 1 on fold (long).

- Cut 1 Back 2 on fold (long).

- Cut 2 Sleeve 9 (long).

- Cut 2 rectangles 3˝ × 6˝ for the
  front facings.

- Cut 1 bias strip for neckline
  trim 1¾˝ × 21¾˝.

Interfacing

- Cut 1 rectangle 2˝ × 3˝.

- Read through all the project instructions before beginning to sew.

- A ⅜″ seam allowance is included on the pattern.

- A 1″ hem is included on the pattern.

- Refer to your sewing machine manual if you aren't sure of the best settings for sewing knits.

- Use a ball point or jersey needle.

- Backstitch at the beginning and end of each seam.

- Press after sewing each seam.

Making the Front Opening

1. On the wrong side of the shirt front, mark a line from the neck down the center front the length listed below for the size you've chosen; then draw a ¼″-wide box around the center line. *Figure A*

12 mos: 3⅞″

18 mos: 4″

24 mos: 4⅛″

3 yrs: 4¼″

4 yrs: 4⅜″

5 yrs: 4½″

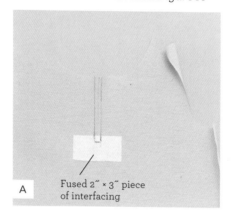

A

Fused 2″ × 3″ piece of interfacing

2. Follow the manufacturer's instructions to fuse the 2″ × 3″ piece of interfacing to the wrong side of the shirt front, centered across the bottom of the drawn line. If you can't see the drawn line easily, redraw it on the interfacing. *Figure A*

3. Cut away the fabric just inside the outer line. *Figure B*

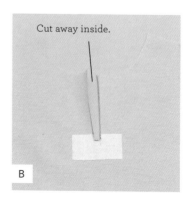

Cut away inside.

B

4. Fold the 2 front facing pieces in half lengthwise, wrong sides together, and press. *Figure C*

5. Pin a folded front facing to the stitched opening, right sides together, aligning the raw edges. Stitch the facing to the shirt front along the opening with a ⅜″ seam allowance, stitching ¼″ past the bottom of the opening. Stitch the other facing in the same manner. *Figure D*

6. Clip from the bottom of the opening to the bottom of the stitching line at both bottom corners. *Figure E*

7. Fold over both facings to the wrong side of the shirt front and press. Press the bottom of the opening over ¼″ to the wrong side as well. *Figure F*

8. From the wrong side of the shirt front, fold both facings toward the center, overlapping them. Stitch across the bottom of the opening from the base of 1 facing seam to the other. *Figure G*

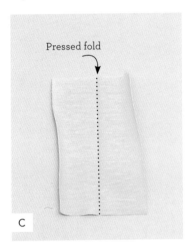

Pressed fold

C

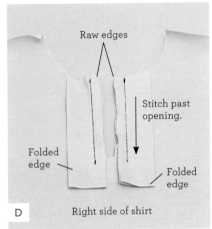

Raw edges

Stitch past opening.

Folded edge

Folded edge

D   Right side of shirt

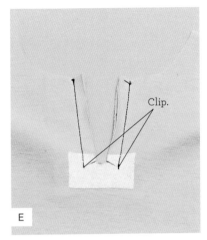

Clip.

E

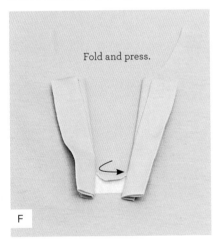

Fold and press.

F

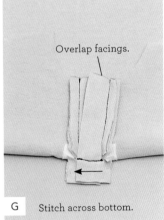

Overlap facings.

G   Stitch across bottom.

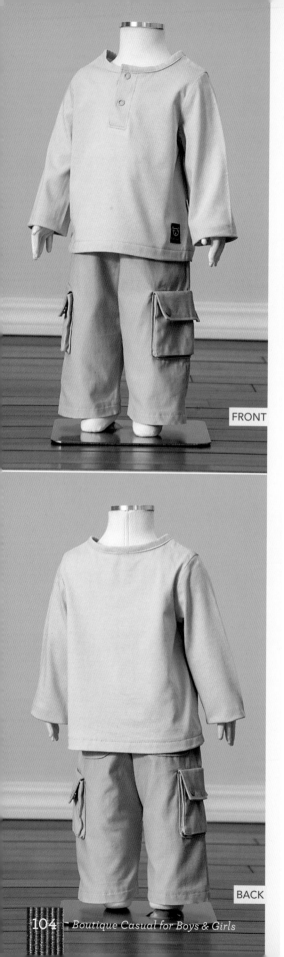

FRONT

BACK

9. From the right side of the shirt front, edgestitch all around the opening, pivoting at the bottom corners. *Figure H*

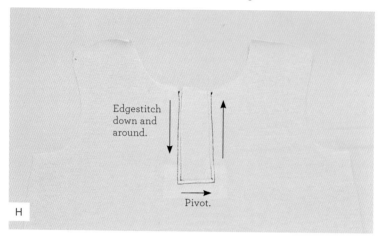

Edgestitch down and around.

Pivot.

H

10. Refer to Making Bias Strips (page 10) to fold the bias strip for the neckline, first folding a short end of the strip in ⅜˝ to the wrong side. *Figure I*

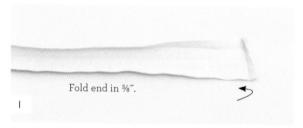

Fold end in ⅜˝.

I

11. Refer to Trimming with Bias Strips (page 11) to enclose the neckline with the folded bias strip. Align the folded end with the opening, pin in place, and sew all around the neckline. Stop stitching close to the end, and trim any excess bias, leaving a little bit to fold under. Stitch to the end. *Figure J*

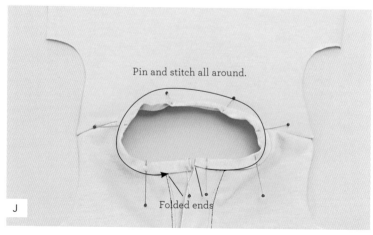

Pin and stitch all around.

Folded ends

J

Connecting the Sleeves and Sides

1. Follow Steps 2–4 for the Double-Button Hooded Jacket (Making the Jacket Body and Lining, page 79) to attach the sleeves to the shirt at the armholes.

2. Follow Steps 5 and 6 for the Double-Button Hooded Jacket (Making the Jacket Body and Lining, page 79) to stitch the side seams on the sleeves and shirt.

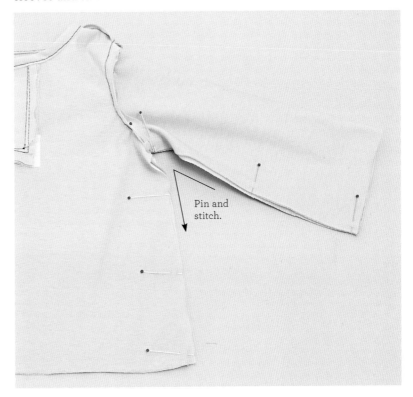

Pin and stitch.

Finishing the Shirt

1. Sew the sleeve hem (see Sewing a Hem, page 15). Sew the shirt hem, but fold only ½˝ for each fold.

2. Make 2 buttonholes on the front opening (see Making Buttonholes, page 12). Center the buttonholes on the opening, placing the first buttonhole just below the neck trim, and the second halfway between the first buttonhole and the bottom of the opening. Sew on the buttons. Or, attach the snaps.

LONG SLEEVE T-SHIRT INSPIRATION

Coordinating Outfits

About the Author

SUE KIM lives in Manitoba with her three lovely children and husband. You can find her latest designs on her website, ithinksew.com. She started sewing when she was ten and has always had a passion for crafts. Originally she earned a master's degree in ancient Asian literature. However, she kept sewing and designing as a hobby until she was asked to be a sewing instructor at a Jo-Ann fabric store. That expanded into requests to teach in several quilt shops, which led to her starting her own pattern business. Her first patterns were for small bags and clutches. Now, most of the patterns Sue sells are downloadable PDF patterns. She always has countless ideas; her sketchbook is never empty!

Sue's fabrics can be viewed at spoonflower.com/profiles/ithinksew.

----------------------- *Also by Sue Kim* -----------------------

stash BOOKS ®

fabric arts for a handmade lifestyle

If you're craving beautiful authenticity in a time of mass-production...Stash Books is for you. Stash Books is a line of how-to books celebrating fabric arts for a handmade lifestyle. Backed by C&T Publishing's solid reputation for quality, Stash Books will inspire you with contemporary designs, clear and simple instructions, and engaging photography.

www.stashbooks.com